SpringerBriefs in Finance

SpringerBriefs present concise summaries of cutting-edge research and practical applications across a wide spectrum of fields. Featuring compact volumes of 50 to 125 pages, the series covers a range of content from professional to academic. Typical topics might include: a timely report of state-of-the art analytical techniques, a bridge between new research results, as published in journal articles, and a contextual literature review, a snapshot of a hot or emerging topic, an in-depth case study or clinical example, and a presentation of core concepts that students must understand in order to make independent contributions. SpringerBriefs in Finance showcase emerging theory, empirical research, and practical application in corporate finance, banking, financial management, behavioral finance, financial markets, social and entrepreneurial finance, microfinance, and related fields, from a global author community. Briefs are characterized by fast, global electronic dissemination, standard publishing contracts, standardized manuscript preparation and formatting guidelines, and expedited production schedules.

Detlef Hellenkamp

Multidimensional Transformation of the Banking Sector

Digitalisation, Demographics, Regulation and Customer Centricity as Key Drivers of Change

Springer Gabler

Detlef Hellenkamp
Baden-Wuerttemberg Cooperative State University (DHBW)
Stuttgart, Germany

ISSN 2193-1720 ISSN 2193-1739 (electronic)
SpringerBriefs in Finance
ISBN 978-3-658-51283-5 ISBN 978-3-658-51284-2 (eBook)
https://doi.org/10.1007/978-3-658-51284-2

English translation of the first original German edition published by Springer Gabler, 2025

This Springer Gabler imprint is published by the registered company Springer Fachmedien Wiesbaden GmbH, part of Springer Nature.
The registered company address is: Abraham-Lincoln-Str. 46, 65189 Wiesbaden, Germany

Preface

Digitalisation, demographic change, and constantly evolving customer behaviour present the banking sector with challenges and opportunities that are unprecedented in nature. Technological progress now permeates almost all areas of the banking sector—and demands not only new ways of thinking but also a profound transformation of business models.

In addition to updated developments, this revised and expanded edition also focuses on the crypto market and Artificial Intelligence (AI), which are increasingly shaping the banking sector. While blockchain-based applications and digital currencies have the potential to fundamentally change existing financial architectures, Artificial Intelligence opens up new dimensions in customer approach, risk assessment, and process automation.

Technologies such as the Platform Economy, Smart Data, Machine Learning, and AI-driven analysis methods continue to blur the lines between traditional banks and new, agile market participants. Competitive intensity is increasing—but so are the opportunities for credit institutions to distinguish themselves more clearly through innovation, trust, and customer proximity.

Customers increasingly expect consistent, personalised banking products and services—regardless of whether they interact with their bank online, via mobile devices, or in-branch. Smart data analysis makes it possible to meet these expectations in a targeted manner. At the same time, customer behaviour provides valuable insights for optimising processes, reducing costs, and strategically realigning the branch network.

Demographic change is also having an impact on the industry: an ageing society, declining birth rates, and competition for skilled workers are changing both the demand for financial services and the structure of working environments within institutions. This book discusses key developments, challenges, and strategic options arising from the interaction of digitalisation, demographics, customer focus, and technological innovations.

It aims to contribute to a deeper understanding, stimulate reflection, and invite discussion.

Note on Terminology

Certain key terms and concepts are capitalised throughout this book to emphasise their conceptual significance within the discussion. This stylistic choice is intentional and applied consistently for clarity. It does not imply that these terms represent proper nouns or formally defined entities.

Stuttgart, Germany
January 2026

Detlef Hellenkamp

Competing Interests The author has no competing interests to declare that are relevant to the content of this manuscript.

What You Can Find in This *Brief*

- Gain an overview of the current (mega-)trends of digitalisation and their effects on the operational and strategic fields of action for credit institutions.
- Recognise the significance of digital developments and the necessary requirements for a continuous re-evaluation of existing business models in the banking sector, including perspectives on selected developments in Artificial Intelligence and the opportunities offered by the crypto market.
- Gain insights into determining factors that generate noticeable relevance for customers, necessitating a customer-centric perspective within banks.
- Achieve transparency on demographic developments and the consequences of an ageing society in general, as well as the specific impact on credit institutions.

SpringerBriefs provide up-to-date knowledge in a concentrated form. They aim to deliver the essence of what counts as "state-of-the-art" in the current academic discussion or in practice. With their quick, uncomplicated, and comprehensible information, *briefs* provide:

- an introduction to a current issue within your field of expertise
- an introduction to a new topic of interest
- an insight in order to be able to join in the discussion on a particular topic

Available in electronic and printed format, the books present expert knowledge from Springer specialist authors in a compact form. They are particularly suitable for use as eBooks on tablet PCs, eBook readers and smartphones. *SpringerBriefs* form modules of knowledge from the areas of economics, social sciences and humanities, technology and natural sciences, as well as from medicine, psychology, and health professions, written by renowned Springer-authors across many disciplines.

Contents

About the Author

Detlef Hellenkamp has been Head of the Degree Programme in Banking Management at the Baden-Württemberg Cooperative State University (DHBW) in Stuttgart since 2010. He also teaches in the Master Finance (M.A.) programme at the DHBW Center for Advanced Studies in Heilbronn. With approximately 34,000 students currently enrolled and over 200,000 alumni, the DHBW is the largest university in Baden-Württemberg.

After completing his studies with the degree Diplom-Kaufmann, he gained around 20 years of practical experience in management positions in the financial sector. He earned his doctorate (Dr. rer. oec.) at the Chair of Corporate Finance and Banking at the University of Wuppertal.

He also has experience in various advisory roles as a member of supervisory and foundation boards and as an advisory board member, and is the author of numerous publications, including the *Handbuch Bankvertrieb | Theorie und Praxis im Zukunftsdialog*, published by Springer Gabler Verlag, as well as the textbook *Bankwirtschaft* (2022), now in its third updated and revised edition.

About the Author

Chapter 1
Introduction and Overview

Abstract This introductory chapter delineates the transformative dynamics currently reshaping Germany's highly competitive banking landscape. It evaluates the profound structural shifts driven by digitalisation, evolving consumer behaviour, and stringent post-crisis regulatory frameworks. Furthermore, the analysis highlights the critical role of technological innovation—specifically artificial intelligence, decentralised finance, and cloud computing—in navigating the increasing complexity of contemporary institutional management and strategic repositioning.

Keywords Banking transformation • Financial digitalisation • Regulatory environment • Strategic management • Financial innovation

The German banking market is a highly competitive market in which credit and financial services institutions compete for customer and market shares in an environment of ongoing, dynamic change. Business models are affected to varying degrees and require adjustments in order to preserve existing competitive positions. Digitalisation, changes in customer demand behaviour, demographic developments, and globalisation are driving **structural change with significant impacts on the financial sector**. Progressive globalisation generally results in the need for regular adjustments and continuous transformation among institutions in competition. Since the 2007–2008 financial crisis, changes have been recurrently accompanied by significantly increased regulatory requirements from banking supervisors and an altered political and social perspective on the banking sector.

Technological progress and the possibilities offered by digitalisation also have far-reaching effects on the entire value chains and processes of the financial sector and thus on the business models of credit institutions; this impacts, for example, the quality and quantity of customer contacts and the digital usage behaviour of customers. The processing of banking transactions is no longer location-dependent, but can be carried out using Mobile Banking or similar services. The COVID-19 pandemic since 2020 has led to a **further intensification of some developments**, for example through the increasing use of digital channels for advisory and for the conclusion of banking products and services.

D. Hellenkamp, *Multidimensional Transformation of the Banking Sector*, SpringerBriefs in Finance, https://doi.org/10.1007/978-3-658-51284-2_1

Artificial Intelligence (AI) is also playing an increasingly important role in this context. AI-supported algorithms enable, for example, **more efficient processes, more precise risk assessments, and individualised customer offers in real time**. At the same time, the financial sector faces the challenge of reconciling the use of these technologies with regulatory requirements and ethical issues.

Customers increasingly expect product and service offerings that are precisely tailored to their personal needs (e.g., sustainability or pension products). To offer attractive financial services, it is therefore important not only to use modern technologies, but also to make intensive use of targeted customer data.

For example, with the use of modern technologies, the crypto market is also becoming increasingly important for the banking sector. While Decentralised Finance (DeFi) solutions and cryptocurrencies such as Bitcoin were long considered a fringe phenomenon, more and more traditional banks are now also looking into the tokenisation of assets and the custody of digital assets. A key challenge lies in integrating potential innovations into existing business models without neglecting regulatory requirements and security aspects.

The use and possibilities of CRM systems, Big Data, and Web 3.0 will also increase significantly in the future. The additional use of Cloud Computing can significantly expand the possibilities for transforming the business models of (traditional) banks.

Credit institutions face numerous challenges that lead to permanently high banking complexity. The management of credit institutions is caught between the conflicting demands of **strategically positioning their own institution correctly and driving forward the transformation of their own business model**—there is no single blueprint.

Chapter 2
Strategic View of a European Financial Industry

Abstract Applying Darwinian principles of evolution and 'survival of the fittest' to the financial sector, this chapter examines the strategic necessity of a robust European financial industry as a pillar of regional sovereignty. The analysis critiques post-crisis 'bank-bashing' and the burden of over-regulation, which have arguably hampered European competitiveness vis-à-vis North American and Asian counterparts. Furthermore, the author advocates significant economies of scale and cross-border cooperation—such as the European Banking Union and the European Payments Initiative—to overcome fragmented national interests and secure Europe's position in an increasingly digitised global economy.

Keywords European Banking Union • Financial sovereignty • Strategic competitiveness • Regulatory burden • Darwinism in finance

We all learn Darwin's theory of evolution early in life and accept—as if it were a law of nature—the survival of the best-adapted individuals, companies, or states as survival of the fittest (cf. Hellenkamp, 2018).

In the age of globalisation, states are essentially defined as the fittest by their access to relevant resources:

- **Military**
- **Raw materials**
- **Financial industry**
- **Digitalisation/Information**

The first two are secured in Europe and Germany in particular by alliance agreements and diversified trade agreements. Fragile alliances and current protectionist efforts are weakening these factors. How 'fit' is Europe now with regard to the latter two resources?

In the years following the 2007 financial crisis, a pronounced politically motivated 'bank-bashing' started in Europe, which repeatedly counteracts the need for a strong European financial industry and significantly restricts competitiveness vis-à-vis credit institutions in other economic areas.

D. Hellenkamp, *Multidimensional Transformation of the Banking Sector*, SpringerBriefs in Finance, https://doi.org/10.1007/978-3-658-51284-2_2

To be clear: abuses in economic life must be continuously reflected upon in all sectors, and framework conditions must be selectively corrected, including politically. This applies to all sectors, such as the medical, pharmaceutical, chemical, or automotive industries, just as it does to the financial industry.

Germany has been the regular export champion for years. Companies must therefore have the option of arranging extensive and complex financing with either high-performance European or German credit institutions. Otherwise, financing projects by European companies, even those with the best credit ratings, such as Siemens AG, could be regularly rejected by potential credit institutions from other economic areas for non-economic reasons. This would mean that European companies would probably regularly lose out in the context of international tenders for financing, for example, compared to Asian and North American companies. Such a development cannot be in the European or national interest.

The Deutsche Bundesbank regularly proclaims that bank executives should take advantage of the current framework conditions and align their business models with the future. The decoupling of large American banks, for example, from European and German institutions in terms of earnings development and market capitalisation has been significant for years.

The need for critical company sizes in the financial industry is already leading to some well-capitalised international institutions easily complying with the cost-intensive regulatory measures and thereby further strengthening their relative competitive position. A look at the issues addressed by national associations now reveals an extremely operational focus, which all management levels in the financial industry must constantly deal with. In such a context, how are executive board members supposed to set strategic directions and develop visions within the framework of their (fixed-term) management contracts in order to align their business models over 10, 20, or more years? The risk that the supervisory authorities, the administrative or supervisory board will withhold their support is considerable and involves a great personal risk.

As a result, most credit institutions operate within the mainstream and align themselves uniformly. This means that they focus on the externally determined implementation of numerous specifications and details. Consequently, business models may no longer be changing in the traditional way, but increasingly through agile management, where responding to change is more important than sticking to a plan. However, this carries the risk of no longer developing visions, but only making agile decisions. This will result in a **loss of direction**. Employees may no longer be aware of their bank's core corporate goals.

Darwinism in the financial industry no longer means the idea of developing the best business model or the best product, but increasingly the **ability of those who are stronger from a capital perspective to bear the costs of regulation**.

European and national credit institutions cannot adequately address the pressing issues surrounding the forward-looking framework conditions for a strong European financial industry, either individually or through their respective national associations. Numerous institutions will have **to generate sufficient economies of scale in the future to ensure the long-term viability of individual business models**. The

Deutsche Kreditwirtschaft (DK) should therefore increasingly move away from the previous interest-driven 'three-pillar approach' to issues relating to a strong European financial industry in order to help shape a common European vision. In this context, for example, an active effort should be made to reach a consensus-based European compromise on a European Deposit Insurance Scheme (EDIS) as the third and final element of a European Banking Union.

Another current example is the European Payments Initiative (EPI), an association of European payment service providers and banks from seven countries based in Brussels. The aim is to create a uniform European payment procedure with its own infrastructure for customers and merchants in order to compete directly with US competitors such as Visa and Mastercard.

Such a vision requires, as a *conditio sine qua non*, a clear political commitment to the necessity of a strong European financial industry. In doing so, politicians should also assess the importance of the financial industry in the context of sovereign borrowing and the possibilities of money creation outside the control of the banking system. The political temptation to take a critical and unconstructive stance is particularly strong in the financial industry, as its image is predestined for this and the sector is complex, with banking services mostly abstract.

The developments of critical company sizes of individual companies with regard to the aforementioned state-relevant resources of digitalisation and information are similarly significant not only in Germany but also in Europe. Here, too, selected international companies generate high cash flow. As international champions, they are shaping further digital developments and thus our common future in a decisive manner. For other potential market participants, especially European ones, including those in the financial industry, this will also increasingly raise the barriers to market entry for digitalised business models, for example with regard to platform-/cloud-providers. This makes it all the more important for European financial service providers to start cooperating, for example in the European Cloud User Coalition (ECUC) forum, in order to generate their own strong market position in the existing competitive environment.

Reference

Hellenkamp, D. (2018). *Finanzindustrie ohne Kompass – It's the missing vision, stupid.* https://www.springerprofessional.de. (Chapter 2 "Strategic View of a European Financial Industry" taken from this).

Chapter 3
Digital Transformation in the Banking Sector

Abstract This chapter examines the multidimensional impact of digital transformation on the contemporary banking sector. It evaluates how a confluence of emerging technologies—including artificial intelligence, blockchain, and cloud computing—is reshaping financial value chains and intensifying competition from non-bank actors such as Big Tech and fintech firms. The analysis further explores shifting paradigms of digital usage behaviour across generations, the transition from multichannel to seamless omnichannel banking, and the critical role of data analytics in fostering customer centricity. Finally, the author discusses the strategic evolution of banking business models within the platform economy, emphasising the necessity of digital resilience and regulatory compliance in an increasingly decentralised financial ecosystem.

Keywords Digital transformation · Omnichannel banking · Platform economy · Big data analytics · Financial technology (FinTech) · Digital resilience

Digital Ecosystems, Artificial Intelligence (AI), the Internet of Things (IoT), Big Data, Behavioural Analytics, Cloud Banking, Quantum Computing, Crowdfunding, New Payment Models, Social Media, Blockchain Technology, and collaborative working methods are examples of technological developments whose impacts and resultant strategic implications are currently being discussed within credit institutions. Technological trends are accompanied by regulatory developments that increasingly enable new market participants to take over parts of the established value chains of commercial banks. This further intensifies competition in the financial industry.

For example, the EU Payment Services Directive II (PSD2) has established a uniform legal framework in the EU single market for internet and mobile payments since 2018. According to this directive, account-holding payment service providers—such as savings banks (Sparkassen) or cooperative banks (Volksbanken)—must provide third-party service providers (e.g., FinTechs) with access to their customers' information free of charge, enabling them to access the customers' payment accounts (Open Banking).

D. Hellenkamp, *Multidimensional Transformation of the Banking Sector*, SpringerBriefs in Finance, https://doi.org/10.1007/978-3-658-51284-2_3

In 2024, this was supplemented by the adoption of the EU Directive on Open Finance, which extends to financial sectors such as insurance, pension provision, and investments, and aims for an expanded integration of financial data to promote innovation and competition. FiDA (Financial Data Access) is part of the EU Data Act, which will enter into force in September 2025. In addition to FiDA, other legal requirements must be considered, e.g., the EU General Data Protection Regulation (GDPR), the Digital Operational Resilience Act (DORA), the Payment Services Directive 3 (PSD3), and the Payment Services Regulation (PSR) (cf. Hellenkamp, 2025c). In this context, FiDA expands upon PSD2—which regulates access to payment data—by granting access to a **broader spectrum of financial data, including insurance data and crypto-assets**.

Credit institutions are increasingly competing for customers with providers such as PayPal and large technology companies (BigTechs)—like Google Pay, Apple Pay, or Amazon Pay—which are now firmly established at the customer interface. Legal frameworks can further accelerate digital developments and processes, for example, the requirement for two-factor authentication in online banking and for payments with debit cards (Girocard), credit cards, or PayPal. For years, processes in credit institutions have been increasingly standardised and structured through digitalisation, particularly to reduce costs—for instance, through the outsourcing of securities processing (e.g., to Deutsche WertpapierService Bank AG (dwpbank)), printing or mail services.

Recent studies confirm that BigTechs have now achieved substantial market shares in payment transactions and consumer loans, which further increases the competitive pressure on traditional credit institutions (cf. Melches, C. & Peters, M., 2024, p. 4). Credit institutions, tech providers, FinTechs, and neo-brokers are developing innovative business fields in the established banking market using technical possibilities, which in some cases differ significantly from conventional risk–return profiles. From the customer's perspective, this is gradually creating a process in which the boundaries between traditional banking transactions and new providers—such as insurance companies, or technology corporations (e.g., Google, Amazon, Facebook, Apple)—are increasingly blurring (cf. Gomber, P. et al., 2018).

These technical implementations significantly affect the IT infrastructure and architecture of the institutions. The high investments in digitalisation are partially refinanced through savings—for example, through standardisation, automation, and simplification of products, structures, and processes.

Furthermore, technological progress in the financial sector has far-reaching effects, particularly on digital usage behaviour, customer interactions, and the business models of credit institutions (cf. Glaser, C., 2022, pp. 1–23).

3.1 Digital Usage Behaviour and Its Impact on Banking Transactions

The discourse surrounding digitalisation is now increasingly focused on the behaviour and expectations of bank customers. Customers live as Digital Immigrants in an increasingly digitalised world—their successors, the Digital Natives, are growing up with an intuitive grasp of digital media. Both groups exhibit constantly changing patterns of demand for banking products and services.

Digital Immigrants tend to have greater reservations about digital banking services. They more frequently prefer traditional banking services, such as personal contact in customer care, as they were socialised in a time when digitalisation did not shape private or professional life to a comparable extent. However, studies show that there is also a growing willingness among Digital Immigrants to adopt digital services (cf. Bitkom, 2023, p. 13).

Digital Natives, in contrast, have grown up in a digitally shaped world. They have an **intuitive relationship with digital banking services and expect a user-friendly, constantly available, and technologically mature banking service**.

Credit institutions must therefore specifically target both customer groups to remain successful in the long term.

From a banking perspective, it is therefore necessary to weigh the extent to which traditional banking services should be continued or expanded, while simultaneously developing the digital product portfolio in a targeted manner to effectively appeal to the Digital Natives group.

The broad spectrum of challenges for the banking sector arising from the different demand patterns of Digital Natives (1) and Digital Immigrants (2) is illustrated by the following examples:

- Access to banking services preferred digitally (1) versus personal branch visit (2)
- Ad hoc problem-solving via chatbots or online forums is sufficient (1) versus personal advisory (2)
- Trust in digital security measures (1) versus security concerns about digital banking services (2)
- Expectation of 24/7 omnichannel access (1) versus adherence to opening hours and locations (2)

A current challenge is posed by the so-called Generation Alpha, whose usage behaviour is even more strongly defined by native digital interactions. A comprehensive omnichannel presence is therefore becoming increasingly indispensable for credit institutions.

The COVID-19 pandemic has permanently accelerated digital usage behaviour worldwide and further increased the demand for the availability of digital banking services. During the lockdown phases, modern industrial societies were required to substitute formerly analogue processes with digital ones. Today, customers expect central banking products to be available 24/7, regardless of time or location (cf. Moden, N. & Neufeld, P., 2020).

Banking transactions are increasingly processed via the internet. Many credit institutions have already reacted with a significant reduction in their branch networks. Web 2.0 enables users—both banks and customers—not only to consume information but also to create their own content. Furthermore, the next stage of development, the Semantic Web (Web 3.0), will be characterised by the flexible, semantic linking of information.

This third stage of the internet is even more networked and integrates new technologies such as machine learning, natural language processing, and autonomous interaction systems.

Web 3.0 represents a further stage in the development of the World Wide Web. It is based on **blockchain technology and implies the concepts of technological decentralisation and a token-based economy**. Furthermore, it places particular emphasis on interoperability and data protection.

This technology increasingly enables users to retain control over their own data and online activities rather than entrusting them to third parties. Web 3.0 thus opens up new possibilities for direct transactions between customers and credit institutions. Banks can thereby reduce costs and increase process efficiency, while customers gain increased transparency and control over their financial activities.

In addition, personalised offerings can address customer needs more precisely, which can contribute to a sustainable strengthening of customer relationships (cf. Bhatia, M., 2022, pp. 91–106).

Web 3.0 opens up a multitude of application possibilities to optimise processes and strengthen customer relationships in the banking sector. Examples include Decentralised Finance (DeFi) solutions (with higher security, data control, and transparency), decentralised identities (privacy-protecting identity management), decentralised data management (protection and control of customer data), automated processes (e.g., via smart contracts), and increased security of financial transactions through the use of cryptographic and decentralised technologies.

Nevertheless, the implementation of Web 3.0 technologies in the banking sector brings considerable technical challenges, particularly in the integration with existing core banking systems. Furthermore, it is anticipated that the regulatory requirements for a decentralised web will become significantly more complex in the future.

The usage data of customers—or users in general—are collected in extensive databases (metadata). Through advancing digitalisation, enormous volumes of data are generated daily in companies and institutions worldwide. If these diverse data of a person are linked together, precise psychographic profiles can be created that map essential personality traits of an individual.

The individual, social, economic, and political opportunities and risks of these developments are considerable and demand a critical reflection on their compatibility with the common good in a democratic society. In the simplest case, companies can, for example, identify customers searching for holidays on the internet as a target group for travel health insurance, credit cards, or account authorisations.

The convergence of information, communication, and electronic technologies is leading to ever-new application possibilities—such as receiving and processing emails on a television set or controlling other applications via smartphones (e.g., using smart technologies). The 'Generation Smartphone' increasingly uses banking transactions via mobile applications and expects maximum flexibility as well as seamless access across various devices.

The Monopolies Commission of the German Federal Government already examined current competition issues in the area of the sharing economy and digital financial services in a special chapter of its 21st Biennial Report (cf. Monopolkommission, 2016). In it, the Commission refers to the German Savings Banks Association (DSGV) and the increasing importance of digital access channels: even in 2016, customers sought contact with their savings bank (Sparkasse) approximately 200 times more frequently via the smartphone app than via a branch.

Former multichannel banking has evolved into omnichannel banking, which allows customers free choice of access channel to the bank. Banking products are no longer offered in isolation via individual distribution channels, but are **made usable across all channels**. This creates a seamless and consistent advisory experience, regardless of whether the customer is interacting online, via mobile, or on-site (cf. Jentsch, S., 2016, pp. 369–381).

Digitalisation is thus a prerequisite for the parallel provision of different advisory and distribution channels. The transition to 'digital-first banking'—and in some cases even 'digital-only' banking—is already well advanced (cf. Capgemini Research Institute, World Retail Banking Report 2025, pp. 9–10).

Above all, Digital Natives and, increasingly, Generation Alpha expect a seamless and personalised customer experience, supported by technologies such as AI and personalised algorithms.

Omnichannel banking offers customers a high degree of flexibility and convenience and is therefore of key importance for customer loyalty. From the banks' perspective, it enables a better understanding of customer needs and to address their requirements more effectively. Data analysis and machine learning create the foundation for personalised offerings and long-term customer loyalty.

Furthermore, omnichannel banking—based on customers' digital usage behaviour—can contribute to the automation of processes and the strategic realignment of the branch network to reduce costs.

Numerous banking products and services—such as transfers, standing orders, online fixed-term deposit and loan offers, interest rate comparisons via portals, securities, foreign currency and precious metal transactions, multi-banking financial planning, financial analysis, digital asset management, capital market information, eSafe services, data and limit changes, and PIN/TAN management—are now fully processed online via modern browser-based internet banking systems.

The processing of banking transactions is now rarely location-dependent and can be carried out flexibly and at any time via mobile banking—i.e., using mobile devices such as smartphones.

In this context, mobile payment methods are developing dynamically as an electronic form of payment using mobile devices. Due to the aforementioned EU Payment Services Directive II (PSD2) and the obligation for banks to provide standardised interfaces to third-party service providers, software solutions such as Apple Pay and Google Pay have been available in Germany since 2018.

Fundamentally, PSD2 is an EU directive for the regulation of payment services and payment service providers aimed at promoting the following core aspects:

- Increasing security in payment transactions
- Strengthening consumer protection
- Promoting innovation in the payment system
- Intensifying competition in the market

Intensified competition typically fosters new, innovative solutions. PSD2 enables customers to process payment transactions more easily, quickly, and conveniently, which generally leads to an improved customer experience. Supplementary regulatory requirements also enhance the data security of transactions: for example, since

14 September 2019, online and card payments must always be confirmed by two independent authentication factors from the categories of knowledge (e.g., password, PIN), possession (e.g., card, smartphone, TAN generator), or inherence (e.g., fingerprint).

Moreover, the EU Payment Services Directive II results in more intensive supervision and regulation of payment service providers, leading to greater market transparency.

With the introduction of PSD2 in 2018, the high implementation costs for credit institutions and payment service providers were initially the focus of criticism. Furthermore, PSD2 is considered a complex directive, which is subject to recurrent critical discussion with regard to data security and data protection when dealing with third-party providers.

The use of banking products, independent of time and location, continues to evolve and today includes, for example, purchases with a credit card, round-the-clock cash deposits at cash-recycler machines in banks, and cash withdrawals when refuelling or shopping at supermarkets.

A central challenge for credit institutions is to permanently ensure a consistently high quality of the offered banking services across all access channels.

It is not currently foreseeable that digital distribution channels will completely replace analogue ones, such as bank branches, in the short term. Banking transactions are fundamentally based on trust. Accordingly, humans, albeit with different skill sets in the future, will continue to play an essential role in the banking business. Nevertheless, it is clear that the increase in digital customer interactions, combined with declining branch use, is fundamentally altering the function and significance of the branch.

According to a study by Bitkom e. V. (2021a), 68% of customers consider personal advisory service at the counter to be very important or rather important. Digital offerings such as online banking, banking apps, or online advisory are almost equally important (67%) to customers. Already, 35% of all customers use online banking exclusively.

Digitalisation has profoundly changed the distribution channels of banks—especially in the areas of online and mobile banking.

In the field of AI, generative models such as text-based Large Language Models (LLMs)—including GPT, Claude, and Gemini—are increasingly finding application in automated advisory services, risk management, and customer interaction. These technologies open up the possibility of making processes more efficient, personalising advisory services, and significantly optimising customer service (cf. Aziz, Layla & Andriansyah, Yuli, 2023, pp. 110–132).

In public perception, AI gained broad public attention with the launch of ChatGPT (Generative Pre-trained Transformer) in November 2022. The capabilities of this chatbot from OpenAI are based on a machine learning model in the form of a text-based dialogue system. Since then, the opportunities and limitations of further developments have been intensively discussed in almost all institutions worldwide. ChatGPT thus functions as a prototype and indicator of the disruptive dynamics of future innovations and their potential fields of application.

Even today, chatbots and AI technologies support bank customers in answering bank-specific questions. This can alleviate the burden on customer advisors and allow personnel resources to be directed towards complex advisory processes. Bank customers also have the opportunity to access digital financial advice online via chatbots, AI-supported platforms, or video calls.

The continuous availability of robust automated advisory services can contribute to improving customer service and increasing customer satisfaction.

Through the use of automation and AI technologies, credit institutions have diverse potential to accelerate business processes, specifically reduce costs, and achieve efficiency gains (cf. IBM, 2024, p. 31).

Furthermore, banks can increasingly use social media as communication and distribution channels. Banking services are offered via platforms such as Facebook or X (formerly Twitter). In communications, numerous other forms of social media are used—such as blogs, webinars, social networks, newsgroups, forums, or instant messengers. Through the targeted use of social media and digital advisory tools, banks can reach new customer groups globally and expand their customer base (cf. Del Sarto, N. et al., 2025).

The distribution and communication channels of banks have been considerably expanded and optimised in recent years. Digital developments had a strong catalytic effect, especially during the COVID-19 pandemic (cf. Citterio, A. et al., 2024).

At the same time, significant challenges remain, particularly concerning data protection (the storage of sensitive customer data), the establishment and maintenance of complex technology infrastructures, and the handling of heterogeneous customer expectations within an increasingly diversified customer base.

The transmission of sensitive bank data over the internet still carries significant risks from cybercrime, such as data misuse or hacker attacks (cf. Munira, M., 2025; Board of Governors of the Federal Reserve System, 2023). Credit institutions must therefore implement comprehensive and reliable security architectures and processes.

Conversely, system failures or disruptions can significantly impair customer trust. An advancing shift of banking operational processes to digital channels can thus create a technology dependency that is crucial to the long-term success or failure of a credit institution (cf. Deutsche Bundesbank, 2021).

3.1.1 Selected Digital Developments Transforming the Future of Banking

Artificial Intelligence (AI) Technologies

The potential applications of AI in the banking sector are far-reaching and will be a decisive factor in the transformation of banking business models (cf. Baffour Gyau, E. et al., 2024).

AI technologies enable credit institutions to analyse large volumes of data in real time. This will lead to the emergence of data-driven business models that enable banks to address their customers in an increasingly personalised and targeted manner with optimised product and service offerings.

For instance, data analysis and machine learning can be used to develop tailored credit, investment, or insurance offers that specifically address the individual needs and behavioural patterns of customers (customer service). This leads to more efficient and faster processes in the banking business, for example through the use of AI-based tools for financial planning and advice (automated financial services).

In the development of digital banks, AI will shape data-driven business models whose activities are largely based on integrated digital platforms to provide customers with personalised financial services almost in real time. In the future, this will also include cooperation with FinTech companies to develop innovative financial products and services.

AI will influence almost all areas of banking operations—from risk management and regulatory compliance (cf. Thiele, M. & Dittmar, H., 2019, pp. 163–176; Plenk, M. et al., 2019, pp. 241–258) to fraud detection (fraud management), personnel management, and communication and customer interaction. Banks will selectively leverage these technologies to increase efficiency, quality, and the customer experience.

Nevertheless, the challenges of AI systems must be continuously evaluated, as they can produce errors and harbour decision-making risks. Credit institutions must therefore establish reliable control and monitoring mechanisms to detect and rectify erroneous decisions. This is particularly true because AI systems are increasingly intended to make complex and business-critical decisions (cf. Glaser, C., 2022, pp. 72–84).

The Federal Financial Supervisory Authority (BaFin) currently only approves fully algorithmic decision-making processes to a limited extent (cf. BaFin, 2021).

A brief overview of further developments

The integration of new technologies—such as AI or Web 3.0—into existing IT infrastructures continues to pose considerable challenges for credit institutions. In particular, regulatory requirements for digital security and data protection, as anchored in the EU Regulation on Digital Operational Resilience (Digital Operational Resilience Act—DORA), force significant investments in cybersecurity and compliance (cf. Regulation (EU) 2022/2554 of the European Parliament and of the Council of 14 December 2022 on digital operational resilience for the financial sector).

Virtual Reality and Augmented Reality

Credit institutions could increasingly integrate virtual environments—for instance, by means of Virtual Reality (VR) and Augmented Reality (AR)—into their customer interaction in the future. Customers experience immersive advisory situations in which illusory stimuli create a realistic perception of the digital environment.

Current developments show that financial institutions are already offering virtual branches and advisory rooms where customers can experience and better understand complex financial products in interactive environments. This increases transparency and strengthens trust in digital financial solutions (cf. Deloitte, 2023, p. 7).

Blockchain Technology

One of the best-known Distributed Ledger Technologies (DLTs) is the blockchain, which is often used as a synonym for DLT, although other DLT architectures with different validation and storage mechanisms exist.

The blockchain is particularly relevant in the context of Industry 4.0, for example in the networking of machines, production processes, and automated control systems. It enables machine-to-machine communication and autonomous payment processes without human intervention.

Concepts such as the Machine-to-Machine (M2M) Economy and the Internet of Things (IoT) rely on real-time transactions, which in turn require a comprehensive 5G and fibre-optic infrastructure (cf. Abdulrahman, Y., 2022, pp. 41–66; 67–93).

Blockchain technology will also find increasing application in the banking sector, for example in the secure and transparent processing of financial transactions or in the tokenisation of assets (cf. Jiao, Y., 2024). Through decentralised data storage and cryptographic security, costs can be reduced and regulatory requirements met efficiently.

In the long term, comprehensive development concepts could emerge on this basis—for example for 'Smart Cities', in which DLT-based systems network economic, infrastructural, and social processes.

Biometric Technology

The unambiguous (security-relevant) identification of persons is based on physical or behavioural characteristics. For example, facial and voice recognition, fingerprints, or iris scans are used to make customer authentication and authorisation more convenient and, at the same time, more secure. Banks are also reacting to regulatory requirements of the European Union, for instance, within the framework of the 'European Digital Identity Wallet'.

Gamification

Gamification methods can contribute to customers reflecting more consciously and critically on financial products and services (consumer protection) (cf. Capgemini, 2022, pp. 9–11). Banks use playful elements such as rewards or virtual challenges to promote financial literacy and increase the use of specific offers, for example through Personal Finance Management (PFM) apps (cf. Bitrián, P. et al., 2021, pp. 1310–1332).

Open Banking Solutions

Credit institutions are increasingly integrating open banking solutions, whether platform-based or as part of their own product and service offerings, to provide customers with extended access to financial services—such as loans, investments, or insurance products. Open Banking enables banks to provide innovative financial services by integrating external providers via APIs. This enables individually tailored services to be offered faster, more flexibly, and in a more targeted manner, while simultaneously expanding the product portfolio. Studies show that Open Banking intensifies competition and that customers increasingly expect personalised and innovative financial solutions (cf. Jaiswal, V. K., 2023, p. 19).

Integration of Social Media Platforms

For direct customer communication and the targeted dissemination of content on financial literacy or product offerings, credit institutions are increasingly using social media platforms such as Instagram, TikTok, Facebook, X (formerly Twitter), and LinkedIn. These are strategically integrated into communication and distribution concepts to increase reach and visibility. Social media can, in particular, contribute to acquiring new customers and strengthening existing customer relationships.

Cloud Computing

Credit institutions are increasingly relying on cloud computing technologies to ensure cost-efficient scalability of their IT systems and, at the same time, to increase the availability and performance of banking services. The use of cloud-based systems enables a more flexible adaptation to regulatory requirements and customer expectations (for details see Sect. 3.3).

Mobile Banking

Mobile banking services are being continuously expanded to meet the needs of customers in a networked world 24/7. This includes not only functions for using financial products and services but also options for real-time monitoring and control. Customers can view their finances and accounts worldwide, configure notifications, and track changes immediately.

Transactions are increasingly shifting to cost-reducing and automated distribution channels, for example through advancements in self-service machines, the use of web and video technologies, and the expansion of browser-based internet banking portals.

Customers increasingly prefer personalised and AI-supported applications. Modern banking apps offer real-time analysis, individual financial planning, and personalised notifications. Studies show that mobile banking is now the preferred access channel for many customers and is a decisive factor for the competitiveness of credit institutions (cf. Jahan, A. S. & Sazu, M. H., 2022).

3.2 Customer Focus in a Digital World

Customer loyalty is not created by technological innovation alone, but by the interplay with the existing product portfolio and the personal competence of a bank. Credit institutions are increasingly facing the challenge of integrating their digital and physical banking offerings to maintain customer relationships in the digital world.

Digitally operating competitors are selectively focusing on parts of the value chains of credit institutions to gain market share at lower costs—for example, PayPal as a provider of an online payment system. Furthermore, so-called non-banks, such as retailers, telecommunications companies, or internet platforms, offer selected deposit products, consumer loans, or payment services in the core business of banks.

No uniform concept for aligning banks with digital customer contact exists. The business models of the institutions vary significantly and are, in some cases, subject to short-term strategic adjustments—for instance, regarding branch concepts. Credit institutions are repeatedly criticised for business models that are not sufficiently customer-oriented.

However, this is usually not due to a lack of insight but to the complexity of implementation. Personalised offerings, chatbots, AI-based customer support, process automation (Robotic Process Automation, RPA), and data-driven decision-making processes are exemplary instruments for strengthening customer centricity.

However, the realignment of a credit institution is disproportionately more complex than that of a (supposedly) more agile FinTech, for example due to regulatory requirements or legacy IT infrastructures. Many core banking systems are considered outdated and inefficient, which exacerbates integration problems with new technologies such as AI, blockchain, or cloud computing. Continuously changing legal provisions and regulatory requirements further complicate processes and cause additional costs.

In contrast, FinTechs often operate more flexibly and are more focused on digital solutions, which increases the competitive pressure on traditional banks and forces them to adapt their business models.

Universal banks—such as savings banks (Sparkassen) or cooperative banks (Volksbanken)—are long-established, complex organisational units that have, in some cases, been offering banking products and services to their customers for generations. However, these products are often abstract and immaterial, meaning innovations are less immediately perceived by customers than, for example, consumer goods.

Since banking products and services are generally not patentable and thus largely homogeneous, there is a risk that innovations are perceived as functionally interchangeable.

An innovative banking product is therefore often positioned merely as one among a multitude of standardised offerings, which reduces customer interest in a specific unique selling proposition.

Against this backdrop, banks and savings banks (Sparkassen) are increasingly intensifying their digital development activities through cooperation or equity stakes in innovative companies. Such product developments can either be integrated directly into the core banking system or embedded into the banking offer as independent brand solutions via interfaces as part of investment models.

One example of this is the introduction of Wero, a European payment initiative by the European Payments Initiative (EPI), which provides a uniform European payment scheme. This initiative strengthens European independence in payment transactions and simultaneously intensifies competition with US payment service providers like PayPal.

Although FinTechs often offer solutions for integration into existing core banking systems or API-based interfaces, these must harmonise with the strategic orientation and IT architecture of a credit institution to avoid creating a 'digital patchwork' in the long term.

Attractive financial services therefore require not only the use of modern technologies but also the targeted use of customer data—for example, through Customer Relationship Management (CRM) systems, Big Data, and Web 3.0 applications.

CRM systems are of central importance for credit institutions as they improve customer communication and strengthen customer loyalty (cf. Brühl, V., 2018). They thus represent an essential component of the customer loyalty strategy by enabling personalised marketing and service offerings.

Application possibilities for CRM systems exist, for example, in customer data management, in conducting personalised marketing campaigns, in cross-selling and up-selling, in the optimisation of customer service—particularly through targeted communication—and in the monitoring and assessment of risks from customer-related financial transactions in risk management (cf. Harmon, R., 2019). In this way, changes in customer preferences and market conditions can be identified promptly and transferred to the banking product portfolio.

The integration of CRM systems with other financial technologies represents a key further development. By combining CRM with marketing automation, Loan Origination Systems (LOS), and analytics platforms, financial institutions can design their processes more efficiently and manage customer contact points more effectively. This integration enables the immediate provision of financial services and contributes significantly to increasing customer satisfaction. The linking of CRM systems with LOS, for example, leads to an automated synchronisation of current customer data, which particularly optimises the lending processes and customer service.

Credit institutions can thus gradually evolve from a product-oriented to a customer-oriented approach; that is, products and services are tailored ever more precisely to the individual needs of each customer.

A study conducted by the management consultancy Accenture in 2017 (cf. Accenture, 2017) among approximately 33,000 consumers in 18 countries and regions illustrates that worldwide about one-third (31%) of respondents would be willing to use banking services from Google, Amazon, Facebook, or Apple (GAFA) (in Germany, 25%). Almost two-thirds (63%) of consumers show interest in personalised banking solutions that take their individual life circumstances into account. Furthermore, 67% (in Germany 58%) would grant their bank access to additional personal data—but only on condition of receiving more intensive advisory services and more individualised offerings in return.

This shows that customers are increasingly willing to accept the analysis of personal data, provided that they receive a discernible added value.

These potential benefits are counterbalanced in the age of digitalisation, in particular, by concerns regarding trust and data security.

According to a study by the industry association Bitkom (cf. Bitkom e.V., 2021b), the trust of the population in Europe (48%) and Germany (53%) towards manufacturers and service providers in the handling of data is high to very high. By international comparison, trust in other markets is significantly lower—for example, in China (11%), Russia (17%), the US (19%), or India (23%).

The Association of German Banks (BdB) points out in a representative population survey ('Security and Use of Online Banking', 2021) that banks and savings banks (Sparkassen) have a clear trust advantage over the GAFA companies regarding data security. 78% of respondents rate data security at banks and savings banks as good (62%) or very good (16%), while only 21% of respondents state this for the GAFA companies (18% good, 3% very good).

A study by the Deutsche Bundesbank confirms this finding and shows that 90% of customers place the highest trust in their own bank or Sparkasse in Germany (Deutsche Bundesbank, 2024, p. 45).

The digital transformation towards a future-oriented business model is thus one of the central strategic challenges in the management of credit institutions (Deloitte, 2024).

3.3 Digitalisation and Its Impact on Banking Business Models

The term digital disruption is often associated with uncertainty about the future. It functions as a buzzword that concisely illustrates that existing structures and processes are continuously being reshaped or replaced by new technologies and business models.

Digital change, although often termed 'disruption', can also be understood as an evolutionary process in which complex economic systems adapt and evolve through continuous disturbances. Digitalisation has been profoundly transforming almost all areas of people's lives for years and is thus shaping the business models of a wide variety of industries. Companies such as Amazon, Apple, DocMorris, Facebook, Google, Tesla, or Uber are exemplary of this.

The pace of digital change is remarkable. The internet as a global interconnected system of computer networks, as well as the use of the World Wide Web and email communication, were only significantly advanced from 1993 with the emergence of the first graphics-capable browsers. Companies like Amazon (1994), Google (1997), PayPal (1998), and Facebook (2004) are—from an evolutionary perspective—still comparatively young market participants. Although Apple was founded in 1976, the market launch of the first iPhone did not occur until 9 January 2007.

Since then, digital technologies have initiated a dynamic, continuous process of change that affects all areas of society—private individuals as well as companies. Digital technologies are thus among the central drivers of digital transformation, particularly in the context of digital infrastructures (e.g., networks), digital applications (e.g., apps, web platforms), and digital potential for value creation (e.g., business models of FinTechs). According to the Monopolies Commission (2016), front-end providers are increasingly advancing towards the customer interface via the digital interfaces of traditional banks by gaining access to mobile and online banking offerings.

A key success factor in this context is knowledge of customer needs in order to develop tailored banking products, solutions, and services. Credit institutions, however, are far from achieving complete transparency over customer behaviour—the so-called 'transparent customer'. Limitations arise particularly from data protection regulations, compliance requirements, and economic and technical framework conditions.

In contrast, companies like Amazon, Apple, Facebook, and Google—some of which already hold European banking licences—have been capturing extensive personal data for years via their digital ecosystems and services such as online shopping, app stores, search engines, social media platforms, and instant messaging apps (e.g., Snapchat, WhatsApp, and Instagram), as well as digital voice assistants such as Siri and Alexa, which are processed in their own cloud systems.

3.3.1 Potential Applications of Psychometric Data Analyses

A study by Michal Kosinski, a leading expert in psychometrics at Stanford University, gained international attention. Kosinski began his research in Cambridge as early as 2008 and demonstrated the far-reaching possibilities of psychological behavioural analyses based on the five-factor model of personality psychology (OCEAN model). This model, developed in the 1930s, is today considered the internationally recognised standard in personality research.

Kosinski demonstrated, using the example of Facebook, that precise statements about individual characteristics and behaviours can be made based on a certain amount of user data. The study showed, inter alia, that:

- 68 Facebook Likes from a user are sufficient to determine skin colour with 95% probability and political orientation (Democrat/Republican) with 85% probability.
- 70 Likes are enough to surpass the human intuition of a close friend.
- 150 Likes allow for a more precise assessment than that of parents.
- **300 Likes are sufficient to predict a person's behaviour more accurately than their partner can**.

Today's users of social networks voluntarily provide companies like Facebook with a far greater volume of this personal information within a very short time.

When companies harness the combination of:

- psychological behavioural analysis (OCEAN model),
- Big Data analytics, and
- ad- and microtargeting (personalised approach),

they open up extensive possibilities to address customers in an even more targeted and needs-oriented manner in the future.

If this approach is also supplemented by blockchain technology—for example, by creating transparent, tamper-proof platforms for the legally secure tracking of ownership transfers—completely new business fields emerge.

On this basis, companies can offer a broad spectrum of personalised products via their own platforms in the near future. Furthermore, they could facilitate the acquisition of these products through individually tailored financing offers—including their own risk assessments of the borrowers—either with their own banking licence or in the role of an intermediary (cf. Glaser, C., 2022, pp. 31–63).

The prospect of addressing around 2 billion people—as in the Facebook example—in an absolutely targeted and needs-oriented manner with advertising, products, or financing (possibly based on their own digital currencies) illustrates the enormous business potential of such data-driven models. Similar potentials can be transferred to other global players like Amazon, Apple, or Google in the context of Big Data and Data Analytics (cf. Walker, T. et al. (eds.), 2022, pp. 3–9).

Amazon, for example, already offers its own payment services and consumer loans in numerous countries, while Apple is successively expanding its Apple Pay payment service to other markets.

Competition in the financial sector would fundamentally change if technology companies like Google, Amazon, Facebook, or Apple were to enter the banking business on a larger scale in the future.

3.3.2 Cloud Computing and Digital Resilience in the Banking Sector

The use of modern information technology is of central importance for the financial sector and will continue to gain relevance in the future (cf. Basel Committee on Banking Supervision, 2024). In particular, the use of cloud computing opens up new possibilities for fundamentally transforming the business models of traditional banks as well. Cloud solutions enable the outsourcing of storage and computing capacities, as well as applications, outside their own data centres. Access to these resources is usually via Application Programming Interfaces (APIs) and can be controlled by users via websites or apps.

Various service models of cloud computing exist. The four central models are:

- Software as a Service (SaaS), where software—such as MS Office—is provided in the cloud;
- Platform as a Service (PaaS), which enables banks to develop applications in a standardised software environment from cloud providers like Google, Microsoft, or Amazon;
- Infrastructure as a Service (IaaS), which allows the outsourcing of entire data centres and the use of a basic infrastructure; and
- Function as a Service (FaaS), where individual functions or particularly compute-intensive processes can be outsourced.

If a credit institution offers its customers, for example, the option to calculate complex financial evaluations on its own website, corresponding requests can be transmitted to the cloud via an interface, processed there, and the results then sent back to the user in real time. This reduces the load on the institution's own computing capacity and enables a fast, customer-oriented provision of the results.

Cloud computing thus offers credit institutions the opportunity to move away partially from their legacy and often rigid core banking systems. This can significantly increase the speed of development and implementation of new products and applications. At the same time, the cloud opens up innovative possibilities for the application of AI and for conducting complex Big Data analyses (cf. Glaser, C., 2022, pp. 113–116).

In this way, banks can optimise their business processes and lastingly improve the customer experience. IT resources can be flexibly deployed and scaled—a significant advantage in reacting to changing customer needs and dynamic market conditions. As technological developments continue at a rapid pace, cloud computing offers institutions access to the latest technologies and resources to ensure their services are modern and efficient.

Furthermore, the use of cloud technologies can lead to significant cost savings. Funds freed up from the reduction of internal IT investments can be reinvested specifically in the core business. Nevertheless, the risks associated with cloud computing must be considered (cf. Bhatia, M., 2022, pp. 135–146).

Thus, impairments to functionality—such as data loss or security vulnerabilities—can have grave consequences for banks and customers. In addition to ensuring data security and integrity, credit institutions must meet numerous legal and regulatory requirements, compliance with which must also be guaranteed by the cloud service provider.

Continuous system availability is equally critical, which can be impaired by disruptions within the cloud infrastructure.

Another risk factor lies in the long-term cost structure: the total costs of a cloud solution can exceed the expenses of internal IT systems—for example, through rising usage charges, scaling fees, or price adjustments by providers.

Cloud services can be used in various operating models:

- Public Cloud (for general use),
- Private Cloud (exclusively for one organisation or company),
- Hybrid Cloud (a combination of Public and Private Cloud models, as required), and
- Community Cloud (a shared Public Cloud for specific user groups, such as authorities, universities, or companies).

Furthermore, mixed forms of these models exist.

In Germany, the requirements for the outsourcing of services and processes—including cloud usage—are specified, in particular, by Section 25b of the German Banking Act (KWG), as well as by the Minimum Requirements for Risk Management (MaRisk) and the Supervisory Requirements for IT in Banking (BAIT).

Credit institutions cannot, therefore, be guided exclusively by what is technically feasible when transforming their business models, but must adhere strictly to the regulatory framework. This includes, inter alia, specifications on critical infrastructures, operational information security, IT emergency management, and the management of relationships with payment service users (cf. Basel Committee on Banking Supervision, 2024, pp. 16–26).

Particularly when handling personal data in the live systems of large cloud providers (hyperscalers, such as Google, Amazon, or Microsoft), clear legal regulation at an international level is necessary—analogous to the EU General Data Protection Regulation (GDPR).

If such regulation is absent, the only remaining option for credit institutions is to use cloud services solely for non-personal data or for testing and development environments. This prevents sensitive banking data of European customers from being processed on servers outside the EU.

Under EU Regulation 2022/2554, the so-called Digital Operational Resilience Act (DORA), additional requirements for the digital resilience of financial institutions will become binding from 17 January 2025. DORA aims to strengthen the resilience of the financial sector against digital disruptions and harmonises national regulations on IT security within the EU.

3.3.3 Platform Economy as a Driver of Transformation

The platform economy is already fundamentally changing the business models of companies in numerous industries. Platforms constitute digital infrastructures that provide institutions and individuals with a standardised framework for interaction and transaction. Central features of these models are economies of scale, efficiency gains, and the potential to achieve significant productivity increases through digital networking. Platform companies typically act as intermediaries between institutions and individuals, offer their own services, or combine both approaches to create integrated platform solutions.

The most significant players in this platform economy include companies like Google, Amazon, Facebook, Uber, or Airbnb—in China, platforms such as Alibaba, Baidu, or Tencent perform comparable functions.

Platform models have also **increasingly found their way into the financial services sector and are steadily gaining prominence**. According to a study by PwC, around 95% of financial institutions plan to operate digital ecosystems by 2026 (PwC, 2021, p. 9). In doing so, banks are pursuing the goal of not only securing existing business fields via open APIs and strategic ecosystem partnerships but also simultaneously tapping into new market segments.

However, with the increased entry of technology corporations, insurance companies, and third-party providers into the financial services market, there is a risk that, from the customer's perspective, the boundaries between industries will increasingly blur and the traditional unique selling propositions of banks may lose their distinctiveness. At the same time, this opens up new opportunities for credit institutions to further develop their own business models in the context of platform-based structures.

A central example of this is the integration of payment and financing functions ('Embedded Finance') into the value chains of online providers—for instance, through 'Buy now, pay later' models or loan offers on digital commerce platforms.

The integration of credit and leasing options into the purchasing process at car dealerships also illustrates this principle: customers can arrange financing directly on-site and receive an individualised solution immediately.

According to an analysis by McKinsey & Company, between 10 and 15% of bank revenues and 20 to 25% of revenues in the retail and SME lending business could result from embedded finance models by 2030 (Murati, A. et al., 2024).

Furthermore, credit platforms can simplify and accelerate corporate financing in particular. The traditional lending business continues to be one of the core activities of the banking industry; nevertheless, the efficiency of the underlying processes is increasingly becoming a key focus. Whether disruptive or evolutionary, digitalisation will profoundly change the existing processes and product offerings of the financial industry. Currently, lending processes in many institutions are still complex and resource-intensive—in terms of both personnel and time. This applies in particular to the preparation and documentation of financing applications.

In the context of growing corporate complexity, financing processes represent only one of numerous areas of responsibility for many companies. As financing requests are often not standardised and must be prepared specific to the institution, the involvement of multiple banks regularly leads to redundant submissions of documents. Information asymmetries between credit institutions and companies often lead, in practice, to companies commissioning specialised credit advisers to optimally adapt financing solutions to their needs.

Price and term transparency, as well as short processing times, are decisive factors for corporate customers with good creditworthiness. Digital solutions must therefore be consistently aligned with these needs. In principle, all financing products can be offered on a platform basis, enabling provider- and product-independent advisory services. Such platform solutions can fundamentally transform the business models of credit institutions, especially if they integrate the competencies of market-leading platform operators from other industries—for example, in the areas of data analysis, rating, or valuation of collateral.

Via Application Programming Interfaces (APIs), relevant data could, in future, be transferred directly into the credit decision systems of banks, which would enable the conclusion of contractual agreements directly via platforms—for example, using Distributed Ledger Technologies (DLT) or Smart Contracts.

The potential fields of application are diverse. In cooperation with supervisory authorities, credit institutions have developed and tested numerous DLT-based applications in recent years—for instance, for the integration of distributed ledger technologies into traditional banking products, for the secure transmission of payment-related information between financial institutions, or for token-based liquidity transfers between banks (cf. Paridon, P. & Smith, J., 2024).

Overall, future business models in the financial sector will increasingly be aligned with open infrastructures that enable end-to-end data and system integration. Collaboration will increasingly be embedded in platform-based solutions, meaning that in the future, credit institutions will require not only distinct digital competencies but also organisational and technical agility to remain competitive.

References

Abdulrahman, Y. (2022). 'The Internet of Things (IoT): Potentials and the Future Trends' and 'The Wild Wonders of 5G Wireless Technology'. In *Intelligent connectivity: AI, IoT, and 5G* (pp. 41–66 and pp. 67–93). Wiley. Print ISBN: 978-1-119-68518-0. https://doi.org/10.1002/9781119685265

Accenture. (2017). *Financial providers: Transforming distribution models for the evolving consumer.*

Aziz, L., & Andriansyah, Y. (2023). The role of artificial intelligence in modern banking: An exploration of AI-driven approaches for enhanced fraud prevention, risk management, and regulatory compliance. *Reviews of Contemporary Business Analytics, 6*(1), 110–132.

Baffour Gyau, E., Appiah, M., Gyamfi, B. A., Achie, T., & Naeem, M. A. (2024). Transforming banking: Examining the role of AI technology innovation in boosting banks financial performance. *International Review of Financial Analysis, 96*(B), 103700. ISSN 1057-5219. https://doi.org/10.1016/j.irfa.2024.103700

Basel Committee on Banking Supervision (BCBS). (2024). *Digitalisation of finance*. Bank for International Settlements. ISBN 978-92-9259-760-3 (online). Retrieved November 1, 2025, from https://www.bis.org/bcbs/publ/d575.pdf

Bhatia, M. (2022). *Banking 4.0 – The industrialised bank of tomorrow.* Springer Nature. https://doi.org/10.1007/978-981-16-6069-6

Bitkom e.V. (2021a). *Digital Finance 2020 – Die Transformation der Finanzindustrie in Zahlen (in German).* Bundesverband Informationswirtschaft, Telekommunikation und neue Medien e.V.

Bitkom e.V. (2021b). *Vertrauen und Sicherheit in der digitalen Welt (in German).* Bundesverband Informationswirtschaft, Telekommunikation und neue Medien e.V.

Bitkom e.V. (2023, December). *So digital ist die deutsche Finanz- und Versicherungsbranche* (in German).

Bitrián, P., Buil, I., & Catalán, S. (2021). Making finance fun: The gamification of personal financial management apps. *International Journal of Bank Marketing, 39*(7), 1310–1332. https://doi.org/10.1108/IJBM-02-2021-0074

Board of Governors of the Federal Reserve System. (2023). *Cybersecurity and financial system resilience report.* Retrieved November 1, 2025, from https://www.federalreserve.gov/publications/files/cybersecurity-report-202308.pdf

Brühl, V. (2018). Banking 4.0 – Strategische Herausforderungen im digitalen Zeitalter. In V. Brühl & J. Dorschel (Eds.), *Praxishandbuch Digital Banking* (pp. 3–12). Springer Verlag. https://doi.org/10.1007/978-3-658-18890-0_1

Bundesanstalt für Finanzdienstleistungsaufsicht (BaFin). (2021). *Big data and artificial intelligence: Principles for the use of algorithms in decision-making processes* (pp. 1–16). https://www.bafin.de/ref/19594552

Bundesverband deutscher Banken. (2021). *Sicherheit und Nutzung von Online Banking* (in German).

Capgemini. (2022). *World Retail Banking Report 2022.* The customer-engagement imperative – What banks can learn from the Fintech playbook.

Capgemini Research Institute. (2025). *World Retail Banking Report 2025.* Attract, engage, and delight – Spin the customer centricity flywheel.

Citterio, A., King, T. & Locatelli, R. (2024) Is digital transformation profitable for banks? Evidence from Europe. *Finance Research Letters, 70.* ISSN 1544-6123. https://doi.org/10.1016/j.frl.2024.106269

Deloitte. (2023). *Banking im Metaverse – die Zukunft des Bankgeschäfts im digitalen Zeitalter?* (in German).

Deloitte. (2024). *Digital Banking Maturity 2024.*

Del Sarto, N., Bocchialini, E., Gai, L., & Ielasi, F. (2025). Digital banking: How social media is shaping the game. *Qualitative Research in Financial Markets, 17*(2), 348–369. https://doi.org/10.1108/QRFM-12-2023-0314

Deutsche Bundesbank. (2021, July). *Digital risks in the banking sector* (pp. 49–64). Monthly Report.

Deutsche Bundesbank. (2024, July). *Payment behaviour in Germany in 2023*. Monthly Report.
Glaser, C. (2022). *Digitale Transformation im Bankenumfeld* (in German). Springer Gabler Verlag. https://doi.org/10.1007/978-3-658-35705-4
Gomber, P., Kauffman, R., Parker, C., & Weber, B. (2018). On the FinTech revolution: Interpreting the forces of innovation, disruption, and transformation in financial services. *Journal of Management Information Systems, 35*(1), 220–265. https://doi.org/10.1080/07421222.2018.1440766
Harmon, R. (2019). Big data and the CRO of the future. In V. Liermann & C. Stegmann (Eds.), *The impact of digital transformation and FinTech on the finance professional* (pp. 225–237). Palgrave Macmillan. https://doi.org/10.1007/978-3-030-23719-6_13
Hellenkamp, D. (2025c, April 26). *Regulatory Agenda 2025 and its outlook: Between complexity and necessity – a critical analysis of the European banking sector*. Available at SSRN: https://doi.org/10.2139/ssrn.5232151
IBM. (2024, January). *2024 Global Outlook for Banking and Financial Markets – Regenerate banking with AI.*
Jahan, A. S., & Sazu, M. H. (2022). Rise of mobile banking: A phoenix moment for the financial industry. *Management & Data Science*.
Jaiswal, V. K. (2023). The impact of open banking on financial services: Advantages, challenges, and regulatory considerations. *International Journal of Novel Research and Development (JNRD), 8*(7), 19–30.
Jentsch, S. (2016). Banken-Technologie – Anforderungen an die Bank der Zukunft. In D. Hellenkamp & Kai Fürderer (Eds.), *Handbuch Bankvertrieb* (pp. 369–381). Springer Gabler, Wiesbaden. https://doi.org/10.1007/978-3-658-06447-1_22
Jiao, Y. (2024). The impact of blockchain technology: Cross-border payments, digital currencies, and financial risks. *Advances in Economics, Management and Political Sciences, 85*, 8–17. https://doi.org/10.54254/2754-1169/85/20240828
Melches, C., & Peters, M. (2024). *Mehr Macht, mehr Geld: Big-Techs im Finanzwesen (in German)*. Finanzwende Recherche.
Moden, N., & Neufeld, P. (Ernst & Young). (2020, July 15). *How COVID-19 has sped up digitization for the banking sector*. https://go.ey.com/4eIDEgX
Monopolkommission. (Ed.). (2016). *21. Hauptgutachten der Monopolkommission, Wettbewerb 2016* (in German). www.monopolkommission.de. (Content: Chapter V, Digitale Märkte: Sharing Economy und FinTechs, Section 3: 'Digitalisierung auf den Finanzmärkten', pp. 409–436).
Munira, M. S. K. (2025). *Digital transformation in banking: A systematic review of trends, technologies, and challenges*. SSRN. https://doi.org/10.2139/ssrn.5161354
Murati, A., Skau, O., & De Geer, A. (2024, July 15). *Embedded finance: How banks and customer platforms are converging*. McKinsey (Article).
Paridon, P., & Smith, J. (2024, February 1). *Distributed ledger technology: A case study of the regulatory approach to banks' use of new technology*. Bank Policy Institute (bpi).
Plenk, M., Levant, I., & Bellon, N. (2019). How technology (or distributed ledger technology and algorithms like deep learning and machine learning) can help to comply with regulatory requirements. In V. Liermann & C. Stegmann (Eds.), *The impact of digital transformation and FinTech on the finance professional* (pp. 241–258). Palgrave Macmillan. https://doi.org/10.1007/978-3-030-23719-6_14
PwC. (2021, February). *Die neue Säule des Geschäftsmodells? Relevanz digitaler Ökosysteme für deutsche Banken – Befragung deutscher Bankentscheider* (in German).
Thiele, M., & Dittmar, H. (2019). Internal credit risk models with machine learning. In V. Liermann & C. Stegmann (Eds.), *The impact of digital transformation and FinTech on the finance professional* (pp. 163–176). Palgrave Macmillan. https://doi.org/10.1007/978-3-030-23719-6_10
Walker, T., Davis, F., & Schwartz, T. (Eds.). (2022). *Big data in finance – opportunities and challenges of financial digitalization*. Palgrave Macmillan. https://doi.org/10.1007/978-3-031-12240-8

Chapter 4
Artificial Intelligence Generates Innovation and Risk Awareness in Banks

Abstract This chapter examines the integration of artificial intelligence (AI) to enhance customer activation and operational innovation in banking. It explores how predictive modelling and behavioural banking insights enable institutions to tap into underserved market segments through highly personalised services. Concurrently, the analysis addresses the regulatory framework established by the 2024 EU AI Act, emphasising the necessity of a risk-based approach to high-stakes applications. The author concludes that the strategic alignment of technological advancement with ethical governance and legal compliance is essential for sustaining institutional competitiveness and long-term customer trust.

Keywords Artificial Intelligence (AI) · EU AI Act · Behavioural banking · Predictive modelling · Financial compliance · Customer centricity

Advancing digitalisation gives banks the opportunity to better understand their customers and activate them individually and specifically. The use of Artificial Intelligence (AI) is crucial for this, even if the industry must keep an eye on regulation (cf. Hellenkamp, 2025a).

Artificial Intelligence provides credit institutions with a wide range of new perspectives for the further development of their banking business—from the detailed analysis of existing customer data to the anticipation of future behaviour. For example, institutions can offer suitable financing solutions at an early stage if they recognise when customers are likely to have higher capital requirements. These and other opportunities not only increase customer satisfaction but also offer considerable potential for future revenue growth.

Numerous studies show that customers react differently to financial products. Factors such as age, life stage, risk tolerance, financial literacy, and personal consumption behaviour play a significant role in deciding for or against certain banking services.

Efficient segmentation, coupled with comprehensive data analysis, enables institutions to create tailor-made offers. Behavioural banking approaches can make a

D. Hellenkamp, *Multidimensional Transformation of the Banking Sector*, SpringerBriefs in Finance, https://doi.org/10.1007/978-3-658-51284-2_4

difference here: **psychological insights into human behaviour and patterns, as well as targeted usage impulses, can motivate customers to engage in more active financial behaviour**, creating a win-win situation. And this is where AI-supported systems offer unprecedented potential for credit institutions that has largely remained untapped until now.

AI-supported systems make it possible to identify behavioural patterns in a multi-banking context and use them to derive comprehensive recommendations for action—for example, in automated lending, personalised account management, Cashflow Forecast, or Fraud Detection. Interaction histories, price sensitivities, risk appetites, and much more can be integrated—enabling a response that is tailored to the current life situation, relevant in terms of content, and creates added value.

If customer revenues in bank sales are generated in an approximately Pareto-distributed manner—i.e., 20% of customers = 80% of revenue—it is not surprising that the majority of work in bank sales has so far been focused on 80% of this revenue performance. The idea of **finally activating the 80% of untapped customer potentia**l is not new.

Apart from the fact that this customer potential may belong to competitors among their 20% of revenue-relevant customers and is already being intensively serviced there, initiatives have so far mostly been insufficiently targeted and needs-oriented. Customers with whom, in practice, there has been little communication for years are difficult to activate using simple selection lists and imprecise approaches.

And what impression is created when these customers, who view the bank as their second or third bank connection, are repeatedly contacted in an uninformed and non-needs-oriented manner? These actions, which are mostly relevant to target values, are also unmotivating for bank sales staff in this form and usually do not meet the bank's own standards for a professional approach.

With the help of advanced analytics, predictive modelling, and machine learning, banks can evaluate their huge amounts of data on payment flows, transaction behaviour, and socio-economic profiles. These can be used to determine which offers customers are most likely to accept or where specific advice is indicated.

AI enables forecasts that go far beyond traditional methods, allowing early detection of liquidity bottlenecks, for example. On this basis, institutions can develop proactive recommendations for action and service concepts. Customers are approached precisely when it is most relevant to them. In this way, AI significantly improves the personalisation of customer care through more individualised services.

4.1 Regulatory Integration Through the EU AI Act

However, with the adoption of the EU Regulation on Artificial Intelligence (EU AI Act) in 2024, it is clear that AI systems used in financial decisions must meet high compliance requirements. European legislators have formulated the requirements for achieving trustworthy AI in the form of a list and have specified their intentions in this regard using examples:

1. **Priority of human action and human oversight, for example, in the broader context of our fundamental rights such as data protection, non-discrimination, dignity, and freedom**. This is to ensure that humans retain control and responsibility for decisions in the development and use of AI systems.
2. Technical robustness and security, for example, resilience against attacks and security breaches, contingency plans, and general security, precision, reliability, and reproducibility.
3. Privacy protection and data quality management, for example, respect for privacy, data quality, and integrity, and data access.
4. Transparency, for example, traceability, explainability, and communication.
5. Diversity, non-discrimination, and fairness, for example, avoidance of unfair biases, accessibility and universal design, and stakeholder participation.
6. Social and environmental well-being, for example, sustainability and environmental protection, social impact, society, and democracy.
7. Accountability, e.g., verifiability, minimisation, and reporting of negative impacts, trade-offs, and remedies.

The legal framework defines a **risk-based approach for AI systems with four risk levels: unacceptable risk (prohibited practices), high-risk (high-risk AI systems), limited risk, and minimal or no risk**.

This results in different possible uses and restrictions for each risk level. For example, AI systems that are considered a clear threat to the safety, livelihood, and rights of people are prohibited. High-risk AI systems include AI technologies that, for example, involve essential private and public services—such as credit assessments that deny people the opportunity to obtain credit—and are therefore subject to strict obligations before they can be placed on the market. The Federal Network Agency acts as the national market surveillance authority in Germany.

While the EU AI Act strengthens consumer protection and ensures fair lending processes, it also means a significant administrative burden for banks. In addition, comprehensive documentation and transparency requirements must be met. And there are numerous such requirements, for example, within the framework of the GDPR or MaRisk. High-risk applications in particular, such as automated creditworthiness checks or risk premium calculations, are therefore increasingly the focus of supervision.

Despite strict guidelines, it is essential for credit institutions to tap into the potential of AI. Appropriate governance and risk management structures help to overcome the tension between technological progress and legal conformity. Those who establish a solid compliance concept at an early stage can combine sustainable customer benefits and innovation. This not only secures competitive advantages for a bank but also promotes and develops customer trust. If credit institutions do not participate sufficiently in the transformation now due to the design effort and, in some cases, considerable regulatory requirements, the effects will probably only become apparent in a significantly negative way after a delay.

Artificial Intelligence (AI) will change our world forever. AI should therefore certainly be considered from a risk perspective, but **our actions should be guided and shaped by opportunities**. In the long term, the ability to offer individual solutions based on professional AI analysis while complying with all regulatory requirements will determine the success of financial institutions in the market.

Reference

Hellenkamp, D. (2025a, January 30). *KI generiert in Banken Innovationskraft und Risikobewusstsein*. Springer-Professional Online. https://www.springerprofessional.de. (Chapter 4 "Artificial Intelligence Generates Innovation and Risk Awareness in Banks" taken from this).

Chapter 5
Crypto Market 2025: Between Euphoria and Regulation—An Area of Tension for Europe's Credit Institutions

Abstract This chapter explores the strategic challenges and opportunities presented by the burgeoning crypto-asset market within the European banking sector. It evaluates the tension between increasing retail demand—driven by 'fear of missing out' (FOMO)—and the significant reputational, operational, and financial risks associated with volatile digital assets. Central to the analysis is the impact of the 2024 regulatory landscape, specifically the Markets in Crypto-Assets Regulation (MiCAR) and the Transfer of Funds Regulation (TFR), which have established rigorous compliance and transparency requirements for credit institutions. The author examines various institutional responses, ranging from fintech partnerships to premium-segment positioning, and concludes that coherent strategic alignment is essential to navigating this complex and rapidly evolving asset class.

Keywords Markets in Crypto-Assets Regulation (MiCAR) • Cryptocurrencies • Digital assets • Financial regulation • Transfer of Funds Regulation (TFR) • Strategic banking

In recent years, the performance of crypto assets such as Bitcoin and Ethereum has been impressive. They have now become an integral part of global financial markets and are no longer just investments for a few tech enthusiasts (cf. Hellenkamp, 2025b).

Commercial banks in the European market in particular are facing the challenge of offering crypto trading to an increasingly interested retail clientele while managing the risks associated with an extremely volatile asset class. The European regulatory provisions that have recently come into force, such as the Markets in Crypto-Assets Regulation (MiCAR) and the Transfer of Funds Regulation (TFR) increase regulatory requirements for credit institutions, which significantly complicates the strategic decisions of these institutions.

Furthermore, the tension between the growing desire of private investors for crypto investments and the resulting legal, reputational, and business risks to which European commercial banks are exposed will be the focus of attention.

With the sharp rise in the prices of numerous cryptocurrencies, interest among private customers has increased significantly. Bitcoin, for example, has repeatedly

D. Hellenkamp, *Multidimensional Transformation of the Banking Sector*, SpringerBriefs in Finance, https://doi.org/10.1007/978-3-658-51284-2_5

recorded price jumps in recent years, generating **attention and FOMO (Fear of Missing Out) among investors**. This has put some banks under pressure, as private customers no longer wish to rely solely on neobrokers or specialised crypto platforms, but see their own bank as a central point of contact for all their financial affairs.

Even conservative credit institutions now have to grapple with the question of whether they should offer trading in crypto assets in order to counteract an outflow of assets. As recently as 2022, the European Supervisory Authorities (EBA, ESMA, and EIOPA—the ESA) warned consumers that many crypto assets are very risky and speculative—they also pointed out that they were not suitable for most end consumers as an investment or as a means of payment or exchange (cf. ESA, 2022).

Nevertheless, in view of the sustained demand from retail customers over several years now and the fact that selected Neobrokers are gaining millions of customers, even previously restrictive voices in conservative banking circles are now calling for greater activity in the crypto sector.

Commercial banks find themselves caught between the requirements of their customers and the risks of a highly volatile and, in some cases, still young asset class. On the one hand, private customers increasingly expect expert advice on crypto investments; on the other hand, many institutions fear potential reputational damage and also see the regulatory hurdles, which have increased significantly since late 2024.

For banks that have traditionally offered classical banking services, a major challenge is to accelerate the internal expertise development in the crypto sector while ensuring that all regulatory requirements are met. The risks are manifold, for example:

- Volatility: Price declines of 50% or more are possible at any time in the crypto market.
- Reputational risk: Dissatisfied and disappointed customers who suffer significant price losses may confront their bank with legal action on the grounds of misadvice.
- Operational risk: Adaptation of IT systems, compliance with strict requirements from supervisory authorities.

At the same time, however, traditional commercial banks' reluctance to move forward also carries risks. There is a clear trend toward customer/account shifts to digital providers, which can also **jeopardise customer relationships in the long term if securities accounts and salary accounts are transferred to Neobrokers and crypto platforms**.

The new regulatory framework in Europe plays a special role:

- Markets in Crypto-Assets Regulation (MiCAR): Provides providers and users with a **uniform, binding regulatory framework in the crypto sector of the EU; its applicability has been fully in force since the end of 2024**. In Germany, for example, banks require permission from BaFin to provide crypto asset services under this regulation. MiCAR is part of the European Union's Digital Finance Package of 24 September 2020, which also includes the Regulation on Digital Operational Resilience (DORA) (cf. Deutsche Bundesbank, 2023b, MiCAR).

- Transfer of Funds Regulation (TFR): TFR specifies comprehensive money laundering prevention measures, including the verification, recording, and storage of the identities of senders and recipients in crypto transactions, and has also been in force since the end of 2024. This significantly increases the administrative burden for crypto asset service providers and requires dedicated data storage.
- DAC8 Implementation Act: Reporting requirements for crypto transactions are being tightened to increase tax transparency (Crypto Asset Tax Transparency Act—KStTG), expected to take effect by late 2025.

The above regulatory packages aim, among other things, to increase investor protection and market stability but also raise the requirements for market entry or the expansion of crypto-specific business models.

In this respect, credit institutions are required to define a strategic orientation aligned with their business model, in consultation with their stakeholders, for example through:

Intensified Cooperation with FinTechs
In view of the complex technology and regulatory environment, banks may seek to enter into partnerships with FinTechs in order to offer their customers crypto services. In this case, the FinTech company takes care of the technical infrastructure, while the credit institution focuses on compliance in the broader sense and customer service, for example. Credit institutions can also use white-label solutions or connect their core banking systems to crypto exchanges from selected tech providers. For small and medium-sized banks in particular, such a strategic orientation could enable faster and more cost-efficient market entry.

Careful Self-Integration
Other credit institutions, especially larger banks or banking groups, are considering integrating crypto trading functions independently, for example through their own broker or in cooperation with bank-owned companies. This gives the institutions the advantage of greater control over the offering and direct access to the customer interface. On the other hand, the credit institution bears the entire risk of any potential technical or strategic missteps and is also fully responsible for responding to volatile price movements.

Positioning in the Premium Segment
Due to the increased requirements of MiCAR and TFR, a premium strategy may be appropriate for individual institutions. In this case, crypto-asset services could only be offered to selected customers, such as High Net Worth Individuals (HNWIs) or Family Offices. Focusing on selected customer groups can help to limit (reputational) risks, allocate advisory resources efficiently, and also generate the image of an innovative and at the same time reputable provider.

Recent regulatory initiatives in Europe, such as MiCAR, have created a good framework for greater legal certainty. At the same time, however, operational and legal challenges remain that could slow down the pace of market integration.

Warning signs of potential price corrections as a result of geopolitical and regulatory changes should not be ignored. The political and regulatory landscape is also inconsistent internationally and, in some cases, difficult to predict. This could give rise to additional risks for the global development of the crypto sector. The volatile crypto markets pose a risk for credit institutions and customers that they may not be adequately prepared for significant market fluctuations. The operational framework for action in the institutions must therefore be clearly defined and precisely structured in terms of content, for example with regard to:

- Forward-looking regulatory expertise: Institutions should establish expert teams at an early stage to continuously monitor regulatory requirements.
- Transparent communication: It is essential to communicate the opportunities and risks to customers in a transparent manner in order to prevent accusations of misadvice and ensure long-term trust building.
- Investment in training and technology: The complexity of the underlying technologies in the crypto asset context requires credit institutions to provide comprehensive training in customer-facing and support roles, as well as maintaining stable and scalable IT systems.

Credit institutions face a strategically delicate decision in this regard:

Investors' growing interest in digital assets is putting considerable pressure on the traditional banking industry to make a business policy decision for or against crypto asset services. **Entering the market without a coherent and well-considered strategic direction poses as many risks as passive inaction**.

The high volatility of crypto assets and the recently introduced regulatory frameworks place considerable demands on compliance, risk management, and digital infrastructure. At the same time, competition from technology-driven market participants increases the risk of permanently losing relevant customer segments.

Sustained growth in demand and increasing market acceptance may indicate that digital assets are becoming an integral part of the banking sector's product portfolio in the long term. However, the resulting tension in the banking sector remains challenging for the time being and requires active management decisions.

References

Deutsche Bundesbank. (2023b). *MiCAR – Markets in crypto-assets regulation, services and activities in connection with crypto-assets in accordance with MiCAR*. Retrieved March 17, 2025, from https://www.bundesbank.de/en/tasks/banking-supervision/individual-aspects/micar-markets-in-crypto-assets-regulation-913886

European Supervisory Authorities (ESA). (2022). *EU financial regulators warn consumers on the risks of crypto-assets (2022)*. Retrieved March 04, 2025, from https://www.esma.europa.eu/sites/default/files/library/esa_2022_15_joint_esas_warning_on_crypto-assets.pdf

Hellenkamp, D. (2025b, January 14). *Kryptohandel: Banken balancieren zwischen Chancen und Risiken*. Springer-Professional Online. https://www.springerprofessional.de. (Chapter 5 "Crypto Market 2025: Between Euphoria and Regulation – An Area of Tension for Europe's Credit Institutions" taken from this).

Chapter 6
Changing Demand Behaviour

Abstract This chapter examines the multidimensional evolution of consumer demand within the financial services sector, driven by shifting societal values and generational transitions. It evaluates the impact of Environmental, Social, and Governance (ESG) criteria, underpinned by the EU Taxonomy and the Corporate Sustainability Reporting Directive (CSRD), which necessitate the alignment of business models with sustainable finance objectives. Furthermore, the analysis explores the digital-first preferences of Generations X, Y, and Z, highlighting the challenge of converting extensive data into actionable insights while overcoming antiquated legacy systems. The author concludes that customer centricity and emotional integration into digital lifestyles are now essential for maintaining institutional competitiveness.

Keywords Consumer demand · ESG compliance · Sustainable finance · EU taxonomy · Generational change · Customer centricity

Changes in demand behaviour usually evolve multidimensionally over time rather than through isolated events. Behaviour evolves gradually and is often recognised only in retrospect.

Banks generally cannot attribute declining customer loyalty or rising price sensitivity to any single determining factor. Rather, various influencing factors—often time-delayed—gradually unfold their effect. As a result, products that were once in demand may no longer be in demand today (cf. Hellenkamp, D., 2006, pp. 144–172).

One example is sustainability: a niche topic for decades, it has entered public consciousness as a result of global climate crises, movements such as Fridays for Future, and international agreements (e.g., UN climate conferences in Paris in 2015, Glasgow in 2021, and Baku in 2024).

In future, customers will expect products to be increasingly sustainable and climate-neutral—also from an ethical and social perspective. Since 2 August 2022, portfolio managers have been obliged under EU Delegated Regulation 2021/1253 to explicitly ask customers about their sustainability preferences (MiFID II).

D. Hellenkamp, *Multidimensional Transformation of the Banking Sector*, SpringerBriefs in Finance, https://doi.org/10.1007/978-3-658-51284-2_6

Sustainable transformation requires high levels of investment—and this is where credit institutions play a key role. **Products, services, and business models must be ESG-compliant (Environmental, Social, Governance) and geared towards new demand patterns**.

6.1 Regulatory Framework and ESG Financing

The EU Taxonomy Regulation has been in force in the EEA since 1 January 2022. It **defines criteria for assessing ecologically sustainable economic activities and is intended to promote private investment in sustainable projects**—a central component of the European Green Deal (cf. Hellenkamp, 2025d).

The regulation has been steadily expanded: in addition to environmental aspects, transitional technologies, nuclear and gas energy, and social dimensions have been added. Investment funds in Germany are subject to BaFin supervision if they label or market products as sustainable.

Companies must explain in their own sustainability reports how their activities are environmentally and socially sustainable—including their information policy towards stakeholders.

With the CSRD (Corporate Sustainability Reporting Directive), from 1 January 2024, EU companies must gradually prepare sustainability reports by 2026. The CSRD replaces the former NFRD as a Directive and is central to EU sustainability policy.

To ease the burden, the European Commission has presented 'omnibus proposals' to simplify sustainability reporting and investment requirements. These provide for far-reaching simplification in the areas of sustainable finance reporting, due diligence in the field of sustainability, EU Taxonomy, Carbon Border Adjustment Mechanism, and European investment programmes (cf. European Commission, 2025).

If ESG criteria influence equity capital requirements in the future, this will create strong incentives for sustainable investment. In 2021, the Glasgow Financial Alliance for Net Zero announced its intention to invest USD130 trillion in climate-neutral assets by 2050.

However, since then, some major players have backed away from these commitments due to geopolitical conflicts, regulation, and economic uncertainty (cf. Jessop & Wilkes, 2025). Nevertheless, the fact remains that banks must transform their business models to be ESG-compliant (cf. Deutsche Bundesbank, 2022).

6.2 Changing Demand Behaviour and Strategic Consequences

Public debates often focus on individual issues, whereas sustainable strategies require a perspective on demand behaviour across society as a whole.

During the COVID-19 pandemic, expectations of customer service rose sharply—especially among 18- to 24-year-olds. A Deloitte study (2022, p. 8) shows:

- 85% of all respondents see customer service as crucial when choosing a provider.
- Customers over the age of 35 see little improvement—many even see a deterioration.
- Younger people are more willing to pay more for good service—and are quicker to switch providers if the service is poor.

Therefore, customer loyalty depends heavily on the service experience—especially in digital channels. New communication and information channels, as well as rising expectations for personalised service, also influence customer behaviour, among other things. Credit institutions are faced with the task of translating these developments into a holistic strategy for the future—otherwise they risk losing touch with customer needs and market realities.

An international study by Capgemini and Efma from 2022, "The World Retail Banking Report 2022", discusses how customer expectations of digital interactions are increasing and credit institutions are unable to keep pace. According to the study, 48% of customers stated that they have **no emotional connection to their banking relationship—and that their banking relationship is not well integrated into their lifestyle/everyday life (45%)**.

The study references 8051 customer surveys and 142 expert interviews with executives from the banking sector (North and Latin America, Europe, Asia-Pacific, and the Middle East including Japan).

According to the study, there is a striking inconsistency between the digital and physical banking experiences of customers. If this inconsistency persists, traditional credit institutions face the risk of losing customer value to more agile institutions.

The study notes that credit institutions (globally) possess extensive digital customer data and information, e.g., financial, geo, and health data, social media, lifestyle, and behavioural data. Nevertheless, 73% of executives face difficulties converting this data into actionable insights; 70% do not have sufficient resources to analyse and process data—and 95% of the world's leading bank managers stated in the study that **antiquated legacy systems and core banking platforms hinder customer-centric growth strategies**.

It is noteworthy that managers in credit institutions and customers often share remarkably similar preferences regarding the sales channel mix. For example, around 80% of customers and managers in the study regard the website as a central point of interaction. Mobile apps were preferred by 91% of customers (77% of managers), while 75% of customers (58% of managers) preferred branches.

Empirical results can reveal changes in the needs and behavioural patterns of customers (people) over time and provide a basis for credit institutions to address them in a more targeted manner.

Tables 6.1 and 6.2 show the results of a study conducted by the Global Financial Institute in 2014 (cf. Cocca, 2014). Since specific characteristics of population cohorts in selected time periods do not change significantly within a few years, this approach can generate valuable insights into the differences in the preferences and values of different customer generations.

The underlying assumption is that generations growing up simultaneously in a society share common experiences, social values, or a similar lifestyle. For this purpose, the terms used in sociology to refer to Generation X (population cohort from the mid-1960s to the early 1980s) and Generation Y (population cohort from the early 1980s to the late 1990s, Digital Natives) are taken into account by attributing different characteristics to these terms.

The Baby Boomer generation (in the Federal Republic of Germany, those born between 1955 and 1969) is not taken into account here, as the characteristics of the changed demand behaviour of Generations X and Y will have a much greater impact on credit institutions in the future. Table 6.1 shows, in particular, study results on the needs, preferences and values of Generations X and Y.

6.3 Challenges for Credit Institutions in the Future

For many years, numerous credit institutions have attempted to determine their strategic positioning through performance-oriented differentiation approaches. Following the financial crisis since 2007, regaining customer trust has become a key factor in sales activities. The clusters in Table 6.2 illustrate examples of the challenges facing credit institutions as a result of requirements that are more closely aligned with the specific characteristics of Generations X and Y.

Credit institutions face the challenge of aligning the orientation and values of their business model with the complex requirements of a globalised and high-tech world, while not neglecting to constantly reflect critically on environmental changes.

In this context, Generation Z customers (born between 1997 and 2010) should also be included. According to a survey conducted by Tink in Germany in 2024, **55% of Generation Z customers place significantly more value on digital offerings than on personal advice in branches**. For example, 29% of Gen Z customers surveyed expect their own bank to provide AI services. Almost three-quarters of this generation (74%) regularly use digital financial management apps, and around 58% would be willing to switch banks if alternative providers offered more attractive terms (Tink, 2024).

Table 6.1 Specific Characteristics of Generation X and Generation Y, Study Results from the Global Financial Institute, 2014

Category	Generation X	Generation Y (Digital Natives)
Lifestyle	Balanced Work-Life Relationship	Strong sense of independence and autonomy
	Career is particularly important	Self-centered and personally responsible
	Autonomy, freedom, and self-responsibility are important	Own self-portrayal and acceptance by peers are important
	Authorities, conventions, and rigid structures are questioned	Behaviour is not aligned with rigid norms and forms. Swarm behaviour is oriented towards Twitter, Facebook, or other communities
Financial Literacy	Better educated than the preceding generation of Baby Boomers	Well-educated and ready to learn new things. Willingness to learn throughout the entire life cycle
	Witnessed the Asian and Russian crises, the bursting of the Internet bubble, or 9/11 events	Lines between education and entertainment are blurring
		View of the financial world is shaped by the financial crisis that erupted in 2007. Disillusionment with parts of the financial world. **Own social environment or the judgement of independent third parties is rated higher than a consultation with the bank**
Consumption Behaviour	Lower loyalty towards a specific brand	Entertainment as a component of demand behaviour is important
	Affinity for new technologies	Visual and aesthetic stimuli are strongly guiding
	Multi-bank relationships and switching banks are used more frequently than by the preceding generation of Baby Boomers	Product recommendations are very important
		Trust in new information media is greater than in traditional media
Other	Part of the collective memory is German Unity, stronger integration of Europe, and the introduction of the Euro	Networking online is very important. Expectation of disclosing and receiving a high degree of information
	Financial crisis since 2007 affects this generation in a phase of life where they can first have substantial own assets	Bank brands have no high reputation and no essential customer loyalty power
	Information overload is criticized, retro-elements in consumption behaviour are rediscovered	Ability to move content from platforms without restrictions is very important

Table 6.2 Selected Challenges for Credit Institutions Due to Changes in Demand Behaviour, Study Results from the Global Financial Institute, 2014

Category	Challenge
Technology	Current technical standards are expected. Customers do not accept institutions whose services do not sufficiently integrate the customers' living reality
Communication	Possibilities for institution/customer assessments (e.g. likes/dislikes) and comparison options should be provided
	Virtual channels are expanded. Customers can be in contact with their institution 24/7 via various communication alternatives (Video-Conferencing, Chat, Skype, Social Media)
Information	Information exchange with experts/networks is increasingly expected in the banking sector. This can consist, for example, of factual questions, discussion/disclosure, and implementation of investment strategies (e.g. Investor.de, Sharewise), providing Virtual Community Banks (e.g. Fidor Bank), and granting and direct settlement of loans via Social-Lending-Platforms between capital providers and borrowers (e.g. auxmoney), or new lending processes. In the Customer-Care area, for example, "Customers help Customers" portals can be established
	Customers with global information access no longer accept asymmetrical information distribution as the basis of a product/service provider's business model in the future. Increasing transparency and access to bank-internal information, such as trading platforms, databases, and know-how, can counteract this
	Information providers and knowledge providers increasingly diverge, as the evaluation of information generates a higher added value. This results in opportunities for credit institutions to develop a structured approach to knowledge (Knowledge Management)
Products	Social responsibility and the question of the meaningfulness of investments are clearly pronounced
Image/ Reputation	The image of the banking sector has suffered greatly since the financial crisis of 2007, which is why values such as security and stability have primarily been the focus until now. Future studies increasingly expect offering associations (e.g. Innovation, Progress, Cleverness, and Smartness) to emerge
	Emotionalisation of the brand will gain greater relevance. Customers actively choose their provider, inter alia, to make a statement by naming the credit institution, for example, because the institution is known for breaking new ground in the financial world
	Investment in building an individual image is required
	Opportunities for credit institutions to set new standards through coherent behaviour as a Corporate Citizen in line with the zeitgeist and social values (Corporate Responsibility)
Strategy/ Organisation	Bank organisations are seduced into acting internally (i.e. inward-looking) due to increased regulatory density, especially because of bank-internal challenges
	Innovation cycles are becoming shorter—providers must adapt to this constant readiness for change in terms of personnel, processes, organisation, and above all, culture
	High demands are placed on the institutional structure of a credit institution, meaning the entire bank management must support the business strategy

References

Cocca, T. D. (2014, July 14). *neXtGEN Wealth Management im Jahr 2030* (in German). Global Financial Institute, Frankfurt am Main. Deutsche Bank AG. https://deutscheawm.com/de/Thought-Leadership/Dokumentencenter/67/neXtGEN-Wealth-Management-2030

Deloitte. (2022, October). *Kundenservice in Deutschland: Der unterschätzte Umsatztreiber* (in German).

Deutsche Bundesbank. (2022, January). *Climate change and climate policy: Analytical requirements and options from a central bank perspective* (pp. 33–61). Monthly Report.

European Commission. (2025, February 26). Proposal for a DIRECTIVE OF THE EUROPEAN PARLIAMENT AND OF THE COUNCIL amending Directives 2006/43/EC, 2013/34/EU, (EU) 2022/2464 and (EU) 2024/1760 as regards certain corporate sustainability reporting and due diligence requirements.

Hellenkamp, D. (2025d, May 08). *Institutional transformation in the banking sector: Multi-dimensional analysis of the impact of digitalization, ESG, demographics and banking regulation on German and European credit institutions*. Available at SSRN: https://doi.org/10.2139/ssrn.5247332

Hellenkamp, D. (2006). *Bankvertrieb: Privatkundengeschäft der Kreditinstitute im Wandel* (pp. 144–172). Josef Eul Verlag. ISBN 978-3-89936-499-6.

Jessop, S., & Wilkes, T. R. (2025, February 19). HSBC delays net-zero emissions target by 20 years. *Reuters*.

Tink. (2024, July 10). *Mehrheit der Gen Z würde bei einem besseren Angebot nicht zögern, die Hausbank zu wechseln* (in German). Retrieved March 17, 2025, from https://tink.com/de/blog/ressourcen/2024-german-consumer-engagement-insights/

Chapter 7
Effects of Demographic Development

Abstract This concluding chapter evaluates the systemic impact of demographic change on Germany's banking landscape and the broader socio-economic framework. Drawing on current population projections from the Federal Statistical Office (Destatis), the analysis examines the challenges posed by an ageing society, declining birth rates, and the critical role of net migration in sustaining the labour force. The author explores the resulting strategic implications for credit institutions, including the intensified 'war for talent', shifting demand for retirement and healthcare financing, and the necessity of adjusting collateral valuations in response to regional migration patterns. Finally, the chapter highlights how technological progress and artificial intelligence may serve as essential catalysts for productivity gains to mitigate potential prosperity losses in a shrinking economy.

Keywords Demographic change • Population projection • Migration balance • Labour force potential • Strategic banking • Social security systems

Demographic change in Germany will have a significant impact on political, social, and economic decision-making processes in the coming decades. The population structures established today already indicate possible effects in the future. For around 40 years, the number of children born in Germany has not been sufficient to replace the parent generation. Germany's population is also ageing as the Baby Boomer generation grows older and life expectancy among older people increases. Without immigration from abroad, the decline and ageing of Germany's population would have been even more pronounced.

In the coming decades, the age pyramid in Germany will continue to change, which will also have a significant impact on the banking system in Germany. The Federal Statistical Office (Destatis) regularly publishes forecasts of population projections taking into account specific assumptions in this regard.

D. Hellenkamp, *Multidimensional Transformation of the Banking Sector*, SpringerBriefs in Finance, https://doi.org/10.1007/978-3-658-51284-2_7

7.1 Population Projections

According to estimates by the Federal Statistical Office (Destatis), approximately 83.6 million people were living in Germany at the end of 2024. Since the reunification of Germany (1990), the population has grown steadily. This **growth is solely due to positive net migration—otherwise, the population in Germany would have declined since 1972**, as since then more people have died than been born each year.

According to the "Outlook for population development in Germany and the federal states after the Corona year 2020" by the Federal Statistical Office, immigration is also responsible for a slower pace of demographic ageing in Germany (cf. Federal Statistical Office (Destatis), 2021b). According to this, immigrants are, on average, younger than those emigrating from Germany. In addition, they contribute positively to the birth rate. The Federal Statistical Office presents various scenarios regarding the projected population development up to the year 2070 in its current 15th coordinated population projection for Germany (cf. Federal Statistical Office (Destatis), 2022). Scenarios 1–3 each assume a moderate increase in life expectancy until 2070 (life expectancy at birth for boys, 84.6 years; girls, 88.2 years) and a moderate development in the fertility rate (1.55 children per woman).

These three scenarios differ only in their assumptions about net migration. In scenario 1, Destatis calculates that with low net migration (average net migration of 180,000 people per year), the population will decline from 83.2 million in 2021 (31 December in each case) to 74.5 million people in 2070, i.e., a decline of 8.7 million people.

Scenario 2 assumes a higher net migration (average net migration 290,000 people per year). According to this scenario, 82.6 million people would be living in Germany in 2070—a reduction of around 1 million people compared to the end of 2024.

Scenario 3 assumes the smallest population reduction. It assumes a high net migration rate (average net migration rate of 400,000 people per year), which would result in an estimated population of 89.8 million inhabitants in 2070.

The massive influx of immigrants in 2014 and especially in 2015 has changed the size and structure of the population in Germany—a positive net migration balance of approximately 1.7 million people (cf. Fig. 7.1, Federal Statistical Office (Destatis), 2022).

As a general rule, forecasts of demographic changes, such as a significant reduction in population and a change in age structure, already point clearly to possible social and economic challenges in the future.

7.2 Changes in the Age Structure

The population structure is influenced by demographic processes: fertility, mortality, and migration.

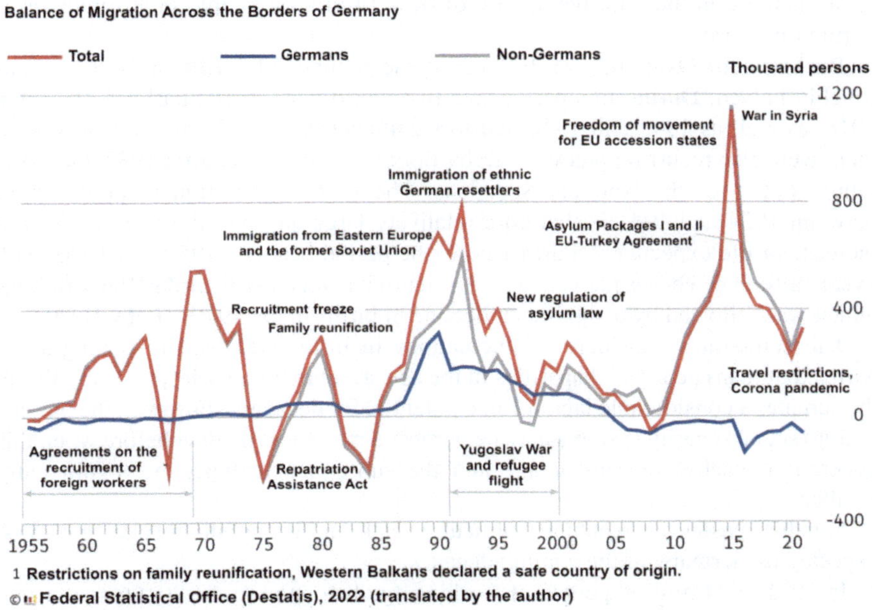

Fig. 7.1 Balance of migration across the borders of Germany

In recent decades, Germany has seen an increasing ageing of the population, which has been accompanied by an absolute increase in population figures.

According to estimates by the Federal Statistical Office, the population in Germany increased from 69.3 million people in 1950 to around 83.6 million people at the end of 2024. This is accompanied by a youth dependency ratio that has been declining significantly for decades and a significant increase in the old-age dependency ratio—both relative to the working-age population between 20 and 65 years—which indicate significant changes in the age structure of the population.

For example, the old-age dependency ratio rose from around 16% in 1950 to 36% in 2019, i.e., 100 people of (working) age between 20 and 65 are offset by 36 people of (retirement) age 66 and over in 2019. According to the 15th coordinated population projection in Germany, the old-age dependency ratio is expected to be between 39 and 56 by 2070 (depending on the scenario).

During the same period, the youth dependency ratio fell from 50.8% to 30.8%. This means that for every 100 people of working age (here: aged 20–66), there are currently around 30 people under the age of 20. Depending on the assumed scenario, a youth dependency ratio of between 31 and 36 is expected in 2070.

Nevertheless, no major social problems emerged during the period from 1950 to 2019, for example, with regard to social security systems and employee recruitment. The main reasons for this are the significant productivity gains of the past and an almost constant percentage of people of working age between 20 and 65, as well as an increase in the total population of over 14 million people in absolute terms during this period.

Background: Over the last 100 years, the number of births in Germany has roughly halved. During this period, the two world wars, particularly in 1917 and 1918, as well as 1945 and 1946, led to significant declines in births. Conversely, there were also recurring phases of Baby Booms, for example, after 1933 due to the family policy of the National Socialists. The senior generation of people born between 1934 and 1941 is therefore relatively large and benefits from an overall increase in life expectancy. Furthermore, the period between 1950 and 1970, with over a million newborns per year, led to a significant increase in births (Baby Boom), which was followed by a significant decline in births in the 1970s (Baby Bust).

The sometimes considerable fluctuations in birth rates lead to demographic waves that (can) generate disparities in the age structure of a society. A Baby Boom thus creates a considerable labour force potential for decades—however, the pay-as-you-go social security systems may be burdened more heavily than before when this generation reaches retirement age and the subsequent cohorts are significantly smaller.

For this reason, far-reaching political, social, and economic changes are to be expected in Germany in the coming decades.

In 2021, 51.4 million people of working age belonged to the 20–66 age group. The Baby Boomer generation in particular significantly rejuvenated the working-age population in Germany in the 1990s. However, this generation is now contributing significantly to its ageing. Currently, over 50% of all people of working age are 45 years and older.

Between 1990 and 2021, the number of people aged 67 and over increased by 58% from 10.4 million to 16.4 million. Destatis expects this figure to grow by a further 4–5 million to at least 20.4 million by the end of the 2030s.

Therefore, when the Baby Boomer generation retires from the labour force in the next 15 years or so, the **labour force potential will shrink significantly by the mid-2030s**. In a moderate scenario—assuming stable birth rates and life expectancy without net immigration—according to Destatis, the potential labour force would decline by around 9 million people by 2040. In order to quantitatively compensate for these losses without productivity gains, between 2022 and 2040, a net total of around 490,000 people between the ages of 20 and 66 would have to immigrate to Germany each year.

7.3 Effects of Demographic Developments in General

The decline in population and the significant ageing of society mean that in many rural regions, the minimum size required to maintain infrastructure is not being reached. For example, even today, some nurseries, schools, clubs, and other facilities cannot be maintained. Retailers, rural doctors, and restaurants are unable to find successors.

Young people and people of working age are leaving their home regions in search of training, an adequate professional environment, and an attractive living environment. Migration and increasing urbanisation in metropolitan areas and university cities are already clearly evident.

The Federal Statistical Office also recognises regional differences in Germany in this regard. At the beginning of the 2000s, the old-age dependency ratio in eastern and western German states was still almost identical. In 2021, the old-age ratio (number of potential pensioners per 100 people of working age between 20 and 66) in western German states was 31. In contrast, the population development in the eastern German states is already showing significantly greater ageing—in 2021, the old-age dependency ratio here was 40.

The different developments are due to a decline in births in eastern Germany after reunification and to immigration to western Germany from the new federal states and abroad, with the result that the ageing process is significantly slower in western Germany. Since the mid-1990s, the old-age dependency ratio has been lowest in the city states, for example, in 2021 in Hamburg (25.1) and Berlin (26.7). Most older people per 100 people of working age live in eastern Germany, e.g., Saxony-Anhalt (41.6), Saxony (41.1), Thuringia (40.4), Mecklenburg-Western Pomerania (38.3), and Brandenburg (37.5).

In the 15th coordinated population projection in Germany, the Federal Statistical Office points out that regional differences will continue to change.

According to this, the number of people under the age of 20 in the city states will increase in the next decade and will be higher than in the base year 2021 until at least 2039. In the eastern German states, the number of people aged 67 and over already rose by around 8% to 2.9 million between 2013 and 2021. According to Destatis, this proportion will continue to rise until 2036 and, depending on the variant, will be between 3.3 million and 3.4 million.

The statutory pension insurance scheme in Germany is organised as a pay-as-you-go system, i.e., people who are currently in employment refinance today's pension scheme. The significant changes in the age structure will place a burden on the pension scheme, as in future there will be a significantly higher number of pension recipients compared to a significantly lower number of contributors. In this respect, the current generation of working people has been urged for years to make increased private provisions for their own retirement, as lower pension levels are to be expected in the future.

In addition, demographic change is already resulting in a partial labour shortage, which (in future) can be partially **offset by productivity gains, for example, through the increasing use of Artificial Intelligence (AI)**. According to a study by Bloomberg Intelligence, up to 200,000 jobs in the banking sector could be replaced by AI applications in the coming years, particularly in back- and middle-office functions (cf. IT Finanzmagazin, 2025).

In labour-intensive areas, such as nursing professions or selected technical and skilled trades, on the other hand, there is a significant shortage of skilled workers, which is expected to increase in the future.

The decline in population will have a significant long-term impact on demand in consumer-oriented domestic industries, such as retail and personal services. Export-oriented companies will compensate for declines by increasing their international focus on growth regions. Declines in demand are not only expected to be sector-specific but also regional. Increasing urbanisation, for example, is leading to positive changes in demand in attractive conurbations or university cities as a result of immigration, while in rural regions, population decline can lead to a downward spiral in demand (cf. Hellenkamp, 2022, p. 88).

7.4 Impact of Demographic Developments on Credit Institutions

Credit institutions are affected by demographic developments in many ways. For example, migration is making it increasingly difficult, especially for regional credit institutions that do not operate in metropolitan areas, to recruit well-trained specialists on a permanent basis and to retain them alongside existing employees at their own institution, a phenomenon also known as the war for talent.

Social developments towards higher qualifications also mean that, for example, over 50% of the younger generation obtain a university entrance qualification and then go on to study in another city or abroad.

Regional ties are thus increasingly dissolving for a variety of reasons, and credit institutions are finding it more difficult, especially in rural regions, to recruit employees who are looking for long-term career prospects in their place of residence. Credit institutions will therefore have to take anticipatory measures, for example, to recruit and retain employees, to counteract age-related knowledge drain, but also to incorporate external measures such as outsourcing and cooperation. Migration within the population will also lead to customers leaving the institutions. Credit institutions must formulate strategic measures for customer retention specific to their institution in order to counteract these developments in the long term. The possibilities offered by digitalisation can contribute to this by enabling banking services to be offered (more) independently of location. Cooperative banks also face the challenge that a long-term decline in customers can simultaneously lead to a decline in equity capital, as many customers are also members of their cooperative credit institution. In this respect, the increased capital requirements under Basel III may give rise to additional requirements.

The declining population and the regional migration and emigration that is expected to be considerable in some areas are also reflected in property and rent prices. For demographic reasons, prices are expected to rise in certain attractive conurbations/areas, while **price reductions or losses in value are expected in parts of rural regions**. In addition, real estate and rental price developments may also be significantly determined by the monetary policy of the ECB.

Collateral is highly relevant for credit institutions when granting loans. For this reason, credit institutions will have to align the value of their real estate collateral more closely with the possible regional effects of demographic developments when granting long-term financing over 10, 20, or 30 years in the future.

Furthermore, institutions that, for example, have a significantly ageing customer base will tend to report a sustained decline in credit demand.

Overall, credit demand from private households, particularly for property financing in new construction, is likely to decline in the long term as the population declines significantly. New approaches to credit demand could arise from financing options for age-appropriate and energy-efficient residential building use, e.g., in the context of a European Green Deal. In addition, product and service offerings in the areas of care financing, health financing (e.g., medical treatments), or the financing of age-appropriate housing developments could also become increasingly relevant.

The ongoing change in the age structure will gradually also change the focus of the product range offered by credit institutions in order to meet the demand behaviour of an increasingly ageing population. The demand for retirement provision products could become more important in the product mix of banks. Future generations of pensioners will have to use up more of their saved assets in order to secure an adequate standard of living in old age. This is why products that build up assets, for example, as part of wealth provision, are relevant. In addition, **products that convert assets into regular income streams during retirement are likely to become more relevant** and attract greater attention. Furthermore, services such as investment advice and asset management are also likely to be in increasing demand.

Credit institutions that are prepared to adapt to the changing needs of ageing customers have the potential to develop new business opportunities. This also offers the opportunity to differentiate themselves more clearly from their competitors. Product and service offerings that are specifically tailored to customer needs can also increase customer trust and loyalty.

From an economic perspective, a long-term decline in population, especially among people of working age, in Germany is expected to lead to a significant decline in economic growth. Theoretically, this can be mitigated or even (over)compensated for by increased capital investment and productivity gains, for example, through technological progress or advancing artificial intelligence in general. Lower economic growth would in any case reduce the distribution possibilities within a social market economy and thus increase the risk of a loss of prosperity for many people (cf. Hellenkamp, 2025d).

References

Federal Statistical Office of Germany (Destatis). (2021b). *Ausblick auf die Bevölkerungsentwicklung in Deutschland und den Bundesländern nach dem Corona-Jahr 2020 – Erste mittelfristige Bevölkerungsvorausberechnung 2021 bis 2035* (in German). www.destatis.de

Federal Statistical Office of Germany (Destatis). (2022, December). *Bevölkerung im Wandel – Ergebnisse der 15. koordinierten Bevölkerungsvorausberechnung* (in German). www.destatis.de

Hellenkamp, D. (2022). *Bankwirtschaft* (3rd updated and revised ed.). Springer Gabler Verlag. https://doi.org/10.1007/978-3-658-37549-2

Hellenkamp, D. (2025d, May 08). *Institutional transformation in the banking sector: Multi-dimensional analysis of the impact of digitalization, ESG, demographics and banking regulation on German and European credit institutions*. Available at SSRN: https://doi.org/10.2139/ssrn.5247332

IT Finanzmagazin. (2025, January 14). *Bankensektor im Wandel: 200.000 Stellen durch Künstliche Intelligenz gefährdet* (in German). Retrieved March 21, 2025, from https://www.it-finanzmagazin.de/bankensektor-im-wandel-200-000-stellen-durch-kuenstliche-intelligenz-gefaehrdet-221165/

Chapter 8
Competitive Situation in the Banking Sector—A Brief Overview

Abstract This concluding chapter provides a comprehensive analysis of the competitive landscape within the German banking system, characterised by its unique three-pillar structure and the traditional Hausbank principle. It examines the profound structural consolidation of recent decades, highlighting a 70% reduction in the number of institutions alongside significant branch closures driven by digitalisation and efficiency mandates. The analysis further explores market concentration metrics, the impact of 'too big to fail' systemic risks, and the distortive effects of implicit government guarantees. By integrating empirical data with strategic insights, the chapter underscores the necessity for financial institutions to transcend 'yesterday's logic' and adapt to the disruptive dynamics of a globalised, high-tech financial environment.

Keywords Banking competition • Three-pillar system • Market consolidation • Hausbank principle • Systemic risk • Market concentration (HHI)

Digitalisation, globalisation, and demographic change are part of a structural change with far-reaching implications for the economy as a whole and the financial sector.

Competitive conditions in the financial system are changing, for example, as new providers enter the market or as existing business models are called into question, either in part or in their entirety, by the above-mentioned determining factors of global structural change. Competition in the financial sector can lead to greater efficiency, but under certain circumstances it can also have a destabilising effect.

The German banking system is essentially a bank-based financial system, as credit institutions, rather than capital markets, play a central role in capital allocation. German companies finance themselves through external financing, in particular through bank loans and, less frequently, through the issuance of bonds. The German banking system is characterised by the **Hausbank principle—a long-term relationship of trust between a credit institution and its customers**.

It is determined in particular by the three pillar structure of cooperative, public-law, and private institutions. In addition to development banks, special features include public-law and cooperative association systems, which are characterised by

D. Hellenkamp, *Multidimensional Transformation of the Banking Sector*, SpringerBriefs in Finance, https://doi.org/10.1007/978-3-658-51284-2_8

Table 8.1 Commercial banking system: share of total assets (%)

Share of Total Assets (%) of the Commercial Banking System as of 31 December 2024	
Universal Banks	82.4
Commercial Banks	45.0
Big banks	20.4
Regional banks and other commercial banks	20.6
Branches of foreign banks	4.0
Public-Law Banks	21.3
Savings banks	13.7
Landesbanken	7.6
Cooperative Banks	16.1
Credit cooperatives	10.4
Cooperative Central Bank	5.7
Specialised Banks	17.6
Mortgage Banks	1.9
Building and Loan Associations	2.3
Banks with special, development and other central support tasks	13.5

Source: Monthly Report of the Deutsche Bundesbank, February 2025—own calculations

mutual division of labour. However, due to their regional business orientation, they only compete with each other to a limited extent.

Every 2 years, the Monopolies Commission, acting as an independent advisory body to the Federal Government and legislative bodies, prepares a report on current competition policy issues, corporate concentrations, and antitrust practice. Competition in the financial markets was last examined by the Monopolies Commission in 2012/2013 in its 20th main report—in the current (24th) main report entitled 'Competition 2022', investigations into corporate concentration, antitrust decision-making practice, and the question of how sustainability goals, especially climate and environmental protection goals, can be taken into account in competition law assessment of cooperations and mergers.

According to this and data from the Deutsche Bundesbank, the aggregate balance sheet total of all banks in Germany has increased over the past three decades from €2.681 trillion in 1990 to €11.043 trillion in 2023. The share of the aggregate balance sheet total in gross domestic product (GDP) increased from 2 times to approximately 2.6 times German GDP over the same period. **Universal banks account for approximately 80% of the cumulative balance sheet total of all commercial banks in Germany**.

Table 8.1 shows the distribution of market shares in the commercial banking system measured in terms of total assets. In traditional approaches, the number of market participants is also regularly used as an indicator of the intensity of competition.

Table 8.2 Top 5 credit institutions measured by total assets in Germany

Top 5 Credit Institutions in Germany—Total Assets and Share (as of 31 December 2024)		
Total assets of all banks in Germany (€ billion): 10,908		
Institution	*Total assets (€ billion)*	*Share (%)*
Deutsche Bank	1387	12.7
DZ Bank	660	6.1
Commerzbank	555	5.1
LBBW	356	3.3
Unicredit Bank (HVB)	290	2.7
Summe	3248	29.8

Source: Monthly Report of the Deutsche Bundesbank, February 2024—own calculations

There has been significant consolidation in recent decades. In the period from 1990 to 31 December 2023, the **number of institutions fell by around 70%, from 4638 to 1403**. This is due in particular to numerous mergers in the cooperative and public-law sectors. Mergers were regularly carried out with the intention of achieving efficiency gains through larger operating units.

According to the Deutsche Bundesbank (Banking Report 2023), the number of branches also fell from 39,750 in 1990 (excluding the new federal states) to 19,501 in 2023. In the meantime, the number of branches, including the new federal states and taking into account Deutsche Postbank AG, had risen to a previous high of 63,186 in 1997.

The German banking system remains highly fragmented. Various concentration measures (e.g., Herfindahl-Hirschman Index (HHI), sum of squared shares) or the cumulative market share of the five largest institutions in Germany measured by their total assets confirm this status. Accordingly, the top five institutions in Germany, with a combined market share of 33% of national total assets, already exhibited the lowest concentration level in the EU as early as 2012. Concentration increased in the meantime, but reached a share of 28% at the end of 2023. One key factor was the significant reduction in the total assets of Deutsche Bank AG. These fell by more than €250 billion between the end of 2016 (€1.591 trillion) and the end of 2023, for example—a decline of 16%. Table 8.2 shows the market shares of the top five institutions in Germany.

In its report, the Monopolies Commission attributes the relatively low concentration to the very low total assets of numerous savings banks and cooperative banks. However, the concentration rates vary greatly from region to region and are significantly higher in some cases.

Competition with financial products in Germany is also shaped by regulatory frameworks. As the financial crisis since 2007 has clearly shown, distortions of competition can also result from implicit guarantees.

Credit institutions and financial market players that are considered systemically important by other market participants benefit from an **implicit government guarantee that acts as a guarantee of continued existence**.

These institutions cannot (from the perspective of market participants) exit the market like other competitors because they:

- are **too big to fail**
- are **too connected to fail**
- are **too many to fail** (i.e., they have a large number of similar business models, and a market exit could lead to uncontrolled contagion effects)

In addition, implicit guarantees can result in further distortions of competition, for example, in the form of potential refinancing advantages. Competition and regulatory measures are therefore intensively aimed at eliminating implicit guarantees.

Internationally, the banking sector is more highly concentrated in all EU member states than, for example, in the US. Within the EU, concentration levels vary considerably.

The reasons for these differences include, among other things, differing historical developments within European banking systems. For example, the German three-pillar system represents an exception internationally. In addition to traditional universal banking systems, such as in Germany and Italy, there have also been varying degrees of separation in banking systems, for example, in Great Britain. Overall, the competitive landscape in Germany remains highly differentiated on both the supply and demand sides. Due to the regional principle applicable to savings banks and credit cooperatives, competition takes place predominantly in regional markets and at the product level.

> The greatest danger in times of turbulence is not the turbulence itself, but to act with yesterday's logic (Peter F. Drucker [1909–2005]).

What You Can Take Away from This *Brief*

- Insight into the tension between key determinants of credit institutions when (re) orienting their business models.
- Insight into the possibilities for the adaptation of credit institutions in the context of ongoing market changes.
- Explanations of digital innovations and discussions of concrete design approaches towards an opportunity-oriented transformation of credit institutions.
- Understanding of the far-reaching social and economic impacts of demographic changes on the banking industry.
- Perspectives on the necessity of a customer-centric approach to address customer needs and expectations, such as a reorientation of products and banking services.

D. Hellenkamp, *Multidimensional Transformation of the Banking Sector*, SpringerBriefs in Finance, https://doi.org/10.1007/978-3-658-51284-2

References

Abdulrahman, Y. (2022). 'The Internet of Things (IoT): Potentials and the Future Trends' and 'The Wild Wonders of 5G Wireless Technology'. In *Intelligent connectivity: AI, IoT, and 5G* (pp. 41–66 and pp. 67–93). Wiley. Print ISBN: 978-1-119-68518-0. https://doi.org/10.1002/9781119685265

Accenture. (2017). *Financial providers: Transforming distribution models for the evolving consumer.*

Aziz, L., & Andriansyah, Y. (2023). The role of artificial intelligence in modern banking: An exploration of AI-driven approaches for enhanced fraud prevention, risk management, and regulatory compliance. *Reviews of Contemporary Business Analytics, 6*(1), 110–132.

Baffour Gyau, E., Appiah, M., Gyamfi, B. A., Achie, T., & Naeem, M. A. (2024). Transforming banking: Examining the role of AI technology innovation in boosting banks financial performance. *International Review of Financial Analysis, 96*(B), 103700. ISSN 1057-5219. https://doi.org/10.1016/j.irfa.2024.103700

Bain & Company. (2023). *Customer behavior and loyalty in banking: Global Edition 2023, Banks' big challenge is the great unbundling by consumers* (p. 22).

Basel Committee on Banking Supervision (BCBS). (2024). *Digitalisation of finance*. Bank for International Settlements. ISBN 978-92-9259-760-3 (online). Retrieved November 1, 2025, from https://www.bis.org/bcbs/publ/d575.pdf

Bhatia, M. (2022). *Banking 4.0 – The industrialised bank of tomorrow*. Springer Nature. https://doi.org/10.1007/978-981-16-6069-6

Bitkom e.V. (2021a). *Digital Finance 2020 – Die Transformation der Finanzindustrie in Zahlen (in German)*. Bundesverband Informationswirtschaft, Telekommunikation und neue Medien e.V.

Bitkom e.V. (2021b). *Vertrauen und Sicherheit in der digitalen Welt (in German)*. Bundesverband Informationswirtschaft, Telekommunikation und neue Medien e.V.

Bitkom e.V. (2023, December). *So digital ist die deutsche Finanz- und Versicherungsbranche* (in German).

Bitrián, P., Buil, I., & Catalán, S. (2021). Making finance fun: The gamification of personal financial management apps. *International Journal of Bank Marketing, 39*(7), 1310–1332. https://doi.org/10.1108/IJBM-02-2021-0074

Board of Governors of the Federal Reserve System. (2023). *Cybersecurity and financial system resilience report*. Retrieved November 1, 2025, from https://www.federalreserve.gov/publications/files/cybersecurity-report-202308.pdf

Brühl, V. (2018). Banking 4.0 – Strategische Herausforderungen im digitalen Zeitalter. In V. Brühl & J. Dorschel (Eds.), *Praxishandbuch Digital Banking* (pp. 3–12). Springer Verlag. https://doi.org/10.1007/978-3-658-18890-0_1

D. Hellenkamp, *Multidimensional Transformation of the Banking Sector*, SpringerBriefs in Finance, https://doi.org/10.1007/978-3-658-51284-2

Bundesanstalt für Finanzdienstleistungsaufsicht (BaFin). (2021). *Big data and artificial intelligence: Principles for the use of algorithms in decision-making processes* (pp. 1–16). https://www.bafin.de/ref/19594552

Bundesanstalt für Finanzdienstleistungsaufsicht (BaFin). (2024a). *AI at banks and insurers: Automatically fair?*. Retrieved February 12, 2025, from https://www.bafin.de/ref/19757872

Bundesanstalt für Finanzdienstleistungsaufsicht (BaFin). (2024b). *Services and activities in connection with crypto-assets in accordance with MiCAR*. Retrieved February 23, 2025, from https://www.bafin.de/ref/19579304.

Bundesverband deutscher Banken. (2021). *Sicherheit und Nutzung von Online Banking* (in German).

Capgemini. (2022). *World Retail Banking Report 2022*. The customer-engagement imperative – What banks can learn from the Fintech playbook.

Capgemini Research Institute. (2025). *World Retail Banking Report 2025*. Attract, engage, and delight – Spin the customer centricity flywheel.

Citterio, A., King, T. & Locatelli, R. (2024) Is digital transformation profitable for banks? Evidence from Europe. *Finance Research Letters, 70*. ISSN 1544-6123. https://doi.org/10.1016/j.frl.2024.106269

Cocca, T. D. (2014, July 14). *neXtGEN Wealth Management im Jahr 2030* (in German). Global Financial Institute, Frankfurt am Main. Deutsche Bank AG. https://deutscheawm.com/de/Thought-Leadership/Dokumentencenter/67/neXtGEN-Wealth-Management-2030

Deloitte. (2022, October). *Kundenservice in Deutschland: Der unterschätzte Umsatztreiber* (in German).

Deloitte. (2023). *Banking im Metaverse – die Zukunft des Bankgeschäfts im digitalen Zeitalter?* (in German).

Deloitte. (2024). *Digital Banking Maturity 2024*.

Del Sarto, N., Bocchialini, E., Gai, L., & Ielasi, F. (2025). Digital banking: How social media is shaping the game. *Qualitative Research in Financial Markets, 17*(2), 348–369. https://doi.org/10.1108/QRFM-12-2023-0314

Deutsche Bundesbank. (2021, July). *Digital risks in the banking sector* (pp. 49–64). Monthly Report.

Deutsche Bundesbank. (2022, January). *Climate change and climate policy: Analytical requirements and options from a central bank perspective* (pp. 33–61). Monthly Report.

Deutsche Bundesbank. (2023a, December). *Tackling the challenges of crypto-assets – the state of play with regulation* (pp. 73–92). Monthly Report.

Deutsche Bundesbank. (2023b). *MiCAR – Markets in crypto-assets regulation, services and activities in connection with crypto-assets in accordance with MiCAR*. Retrieved March 17, 2025, from https://www.bundesbank.de/en/tasks/banking-supervision/individual-aspects/micar-markets-in-crypto-assets-regulation-913886

Deutsche Bundesbank. (2024, July). *Payment behaviour in Germany in 2023*. Monthly Report.

European Commission. (2019, April 08). *Ethics guidelines for trustworthy AI (Unabhängige hochrangige Expertengruppe für Künstliche Intelligenz)* (in German) (p. 17). Retrieved January 06, 2025, from https://digital-strategy.ec.europa.eu/en/library/ethics-guidelines-trustworthy-ai

European Commission. (2022). *EU taxonomy: Complementary Climate Delegated Act to accelerate decarbonisation*. Last updated on: July 11, 2022.

European Commission. (2024). *AI Act*. Retrieved January 06, 2025, from https://digital-strategy.ec.europa.eu/policies/regulatory-framework-ai

European Commission. (2025, February 26). Proposal for a DIRECTIVE OF THE EUROPEAN PARLIAMENT AND OF THE COUNCIL amending Directives 2006/43/EC, 2013/34/EU, (EU) 2022/2464 and (EU) 2024/1760 as regards certain corporate sustainability reporting and due diligence requirements.

European Parliament and of the Council. (2022, December 14). Regulation (EU) 2022/2554 on digital operational resilience for the financial sector. *Official Journal of the European Union*. Retrieved March 14, 2025, from http://data.europa.eu/eli/reg/2022/2554/oj

European Supervisory Authorities (ESA). (2022). *EU financial regulators warn consumers on the risks of crypto-assets (2022)*. Retrieved March 04, 2025, from https://www.esma.europa.eu/sites/default/files/library/esa_2022_15_joint_esas_warning_on_crypto-assets.pdf

Federal Statistical Office of Germany (Destatis). (2019, June). *Bevölkerung im Wandel – Annahmen und Ergebnisse der 14. koordinierten Bevölkerungsvorausberechnung* (in German). www.destatis.de

Federal Statistical Office of Germany (Destatis). (2021a). *Datenreport 2021 – Ein Sozialbericht für die Bundesrepublik Deutschland* (in German). Wissenschaftszentrum Berlin für Sozialforschung, Bundesinstitut für Bevölkerungsforschung (BiB). www.destatis.de

Federal Statistical Office of Germany (Destatis). (2021b). *Ausblick auf die Bevölkerungsentwicklung in Deutschland und den Bundesländern nach dem Corona-Jahr 2020 – Erste mittelfristige Bevölkerungsvorausberechnung 2021 bis 2035* (in German). www.destatis.de

Federal Statistical Office of Germany (Destatis). (2022, December). *Bevölkerung im Wandel – Ergebnisse der 15. koordinierten Bevölkerungsvorausberechnung* (in German). www.destatis.de

Glaser, C. (2022). *Digitale Transformation im Bankenumfeld* (in German). Springer Gabler Verlag. https://doi.org/10.1007/978-3-658-35705-4

Gomber, P., Kauffman, R., Parker, C., & Weber, B. (2018). On the FinTech revolution: Interpreting the forces of innovation, disruption, and transformation in financial services. *Journal of Management Information Systems, 35*(1), 220–265. https://doi.org/10.1080/07421222.2018.1440766

Harmon, R. (2019). Big data and the CRO of the future. In V. Liermann & C. Stegmann (Eds.), *The impact of digital transformation and FinTech on the finance professional* (pp. 225–237). Palgrave Macmillan. https://doi.org/10.1007/978-3-030-23719-6_13

Hellenkamp, D. (2018). *Finanzindustrie ohne Kompass – It's the missing vision, stupid.* https://www.springerprofessional.de. (Chapter 2 "Strategic View of a European Financial Industry" taken from this).

Hellenkamp, D. (2022). *Bankwirtschaft* (3rd updated and revised ed.). Springer Gabler Verlag. https://doi.org/10.1007/978-3-658-37549-2

Hellenkamp, D. (2025a, January 30). *KI generiert in Banken Innovationskraft und Risikobewusstsein*. Springer-Professional Online. https://www.springerprofessional.de. (Chapter 4 "Artificial Intelligence Generates Innovation and Risk Awareness in Banks" taken from this).

Hellenkamp, D. (2025b, January 14). *Kryptohandel: Banken balancieren zwischen Chancen und Risiken*. Springer-Professional Online. https://www.springerprofessional.de. (Chapter 5 "Crypto Market 2025: Between Euphoria and Regulation – An Area of Tension for Europe's Credit Institutions" taken from this).

Hellenkamp, D. (2025c, April 26). *Regulatory Agenda 2025 and its outlook: Between complexity and necessity – a critical analysis of the European banking sector*. Available at SSRN: https://doi.org/10.2139/ssrn.5232151

Hellenkamp, D. (2025d, May 08). *Institutional transformation in the banking sector: Multi-dimensional analysis of the impact of digitalization, ESG, demographics and banking regulation on German and European credit institutions*. Available at SSRN: https://doi.org/10.2139/ssrn.5247332

Hellenkamp, D. (2025e, November 13). *The drivers of digital transformation in banking: From AI and cloud adoption to customer-centric platforms*. Available at SSRN: https://doi.org/10.2139/ssrn.5743322

Hellenkamp, D. (2006). *Bankvertrieb: Privatkundengeschäft der Kreditinstitute im Wandel* (pp. 144–172). Josef Eul Verlag. ISBN 978-3-89936-499-6.

IBM. (2024, January). *2024 Global Outlook for Banking and Financial Markets – Regenerate banking with AI.*

IT Finanzmagazin. (2025, January 14). *Bankensektor im Wandel: 200.000 Stellen durch Künstliche Intelligenz gefährdet* (in German). Retrieved March 21, 2025, from https://www.it-finanzmagazin.de/bankensektor-im-wandel-200-000-stellen-durch-kuenstliche-intelligenz-gefaehrdet-221165/

Jahan, A. S., & Sazu, M. H. (2022). Rise of mobile banking: A phoenix moment for the financial industry. *Management & Data Science*.

Jaiswal, V. K. (2023). The impact of open banking on financial services: Advantages, challenges, and regulatory considerations. *International Journal of Novel Research and Development (JNRD), 8*(7), 19–30.

Jentsch, S. (2016). Banken-Technologie – Anforderungen an die Bank der Zukunft. In D. Hellenkamp & Kai Fürderer (Eds.), *Handbuch Bankvertrieb* (pp. 369–381). Springer Gabler, Wiesbaden. https://doi.org/10.1007/978-3-658-06447-1_22

Jessop, S., & Wilkes, T. R. (2025, February 19). HSBC delays net-zero emissions target by 20 years. *Reuters*.

Jiao, Y. (2024). The impact of blockchain technology: Cross-border payments, digital currencies, and financial risks. *Advances in Economics, Management and Political Sciences, 85*, 8–17. https://doi.org/10.54254/2754-1169/85/20240828

L'Hostis, A. (2025, January 14). *The digital banking landscape is poised for another transformative year*. Forrester Research. Retrieved March 05, 2025, from https://www.forrester.com/blogs/2025-the-digital-banking-landscape-is-poised-for-another-transformative-year/

Melches, C., & Peters, M. (2024). *Mehr Macht, mehr Geld: Big-Techs im Finanzwesen (in German)*. Finanzwende Recherche.

Moden, N., & Neufeld, P. (Ernst & Young). (2020, July 15). *How COVID-19 has sped up digitization for the banking sector*. https://go.ey.com/4eIDEgX

Monopolkommission. (Ed.). (2016). *21. Hauptgutachten der Monopolkommission, Wettbewerb 2016* (in German). www.monopolkommission.de. (Content: Chapter V, Digitale Märkte: Sharing Economy und FinTechs, Section 3: 'Digitalisierung auf den Finanzmärkten', pp. 409–436).

Munira, M. S. K. (2025). *Digital transformation in banking: A systematic review of trends, technologies, and challenges*. SSRN. https://doi.org/10.2139/ssrn.5161354

Murati, A., Skau, O., & De Geer, A. (2024, July 15). *Embedded finance: How banks and customer platforms are converging*. McKinsey (Article).

Oxera. (2023). *An economic analysis of remuneration systems: Effective distribution of financial products*. Studie beauftragt durch den Gesamtverband der Deutschen Versicherungswirtschaft (GDV).

Paridon, P., & Smith, J. (2024, February 1). *Distributed ledger technology: A case study of the regulatory approach to banks' use of new technology*. Bank Policy Institute (bpi).

Plenk, M., Levant, I., & Bellon, N. (2019). How technology (or distributed ledger technology and algorithms like deep learning and machine learning) can help to comply with regulatory requirements. In V. Liermann & C. Stegmann (Eds.), *The impact of digital transformation and FinTech on the finance professional* (pp. 241–258). Palgrave Macmillan. https://doi.org/10.1007/978-3-030-23719-6_14

PwC. (2021, February). *Die neue Säule des Geschäftsmodells? Relevanz digitaler Ökosysteme für deutsche Banken – Befragung deutscher Bankentscheider* (in German).

Thiele, M., & Dittmar, H. (2019). Internal credit risk models with machine learning. In V. Liermann & C. Stegmann (Eds.), *The impact of digital transformation and FinTech on the finance professional* (pp. 163–176). Palgrave Macmillan. https://doi.org/10.1007/978-3-030-23719-6_10

Tink. (2024, July 10). *Mehrheit der Gen Z würde bei einem besseren Angebot nicht zögern, die Hausbank zu wechseln* (in German). Retrieved March 17, 2025, from https://tink.com/de/blog/ressourcen/2024-german-consumer-engagement-insights/

Walker, T., Davis, F., & Schwartz, T. (Eds.). (2022). *Big data in finance – opportunities and challenges of financial digitalization*. Palgrave Macmillan. https://doi.org/10.1007/978-3-031-12240-8

MIX
Papier aus verantwortungsvollen Quellen
Paper from responsible sources
FSC® C105338

If you have any concerns about our products,
you can contact us on
ProductSafety@springernature.com

In case Publisher is established outside the EU,
the EU authorized representative is:
Springer Nature Customer Service Center GmbH
Europaplatz 3, 69115 Heidelberg, Germany

Printed by Libri Plureos GmbH
in Hamburg, Germany